New Immigrants, Old Unions
Organizing Undocumented Workers in Los Angeles

New Immigrants, Old Unions

Organizing Undocumented Workers

in Los Angeles

Héctor L. Delgado

Temple University Press / Philadelphia

Temple University Press, Philadelphia 19122
Copyright © 1993 by Temple University
All rights reserved
Published 1993
Printed in the United States of America

The paper used in this publication meets the minimum
requirements of American National Standard for
Information Sciences — Permanence of Paper for Printed
Library Materials, ANSI Z39.48-1984 ∞

Library of Congress Cataloging-in-Publication Data

TP

Delgado, Héctor L., 1949–
    New immigrants, old unions : organizing
undocumented workers in Los Angeles / Héctor L.
Delgado.
        p.   cm.
    Includes bibliographical references and index.
    ISBN 1-56639-044-3 (cloth : alk. paper)
        1. Trade-unions — Furniture workers — California —
Los Angeles.   2. Water bed industry — California —
Los Angeles — Employees.   3. Aliens, Illegal —
Employment — California — Los Angeles.   I. Title.
HD6515.F9D44   1993
331.6'2 — dc20   92-36423

Para Andrés Martín, Miriam, y Cecilia

Contents

Acknowledgments

The longer you take to finish a project, the longer the list of people you need to thank. First, there is Miriam López, whose companionship I value immeasurably and whose advice on legal issues was especially helpful and appreciated. (Living with an attorney has its good points.) Howard Kimeldorf, a valued colleague and friend, has been involved in this project from its inception (since he helped to conceive it). Few people in my life have been as generous.

Others whom I wish to thank are Mark Chesler, Terry McDonald, Jeff Paige, and Sylvia Pedraza. Jeff deserves special mention for his advice and support at key times in the life of this project. I also thank Tom Gerschick, Cheryl Hyde, and Sharon Reitman for their friendship and encouragement, during and since our years at the University of Michigan.

Special thanks go, as well, to Les Howard and Michael Mc-Aleenan. Les, whom I met in the summer of 1987 at a conference in the Center for U.S.-Mexican Studies at the University of California, San Diego, immediately expressed an unwavering interest in my research. He provided me with encouragement, friendship, and excellent critiques of my work. Mike was a colleague at Occidental College and offered me invaluable feedback, for which I am very grateful. I was fortunate to have him as a colleague while I was writing this book. I received additional valuable feedback from other readers, but none more helpful than Bob Thomas's early in the project.

I spent a very productive year in the Center for U.S.-Mexican Studies, where I was a Visiting Research Fellow. I wish to thank Wayne Cornelius, Director of the center, for his interest in my work and for his invitation — which included financial assistance — to spend time at the center with him and other excellent scholars from both Mexico and the United States. During this time a number of people provided me with important intellectual stimulation and friendship. At the risk of failing to mention someone who deserves acknowledgment, I wish to express my gratitude especially to Luin Goldring, Graciela Platero, Anna García, Lee Dewey, and Roger Rouse. Wayne and Luin both provided useful comments on an earlier version of my work. Lee's excellent computer and word-processing skills were indispensable to me.

During the first two years of this project I received financial assistance from the Ford Foundation (National Research Council) and the University of Michigan. I thank them for their support. I also thank David Axeen, Occidental College's Dean of the Faculty, for his assistance.

I thank the folks at Temple University Press, but especially Doris Braendel, Senior Acquisitions Editor, for providing me with constant support and valuable suggestions. In the process (despite the distance between Los Angeles and Philadelphia), we began to develop a friendship I hope we can nurture. If I have to write another book to do that, I will. I am also grateful to Joan Vidal, Production Editor, for all her help and guidance, and Anne Gibbons for an excellent job of copy editing.

Beatriz Pesquera also deserves special mention. Beatriz, whom I met for the first time at a publishing seminar, offered to bring my manuscript to Doris Braendel's attention at Temple University Press — and she did. I am indebted to her for this and to Doris for reading it.

I am especially indebted and most grateful to the many workers, labor organizers, and others who took the time to share with me their knowledge and feelings about the world in which immigrants work and organize. Regrettably, the anonymity and confidentiality I promised prohibit me from acknowledging them by name.

New Immigrants, Old Unions
Organizing Undocumented Workers in Los Angeles

Chapter 1

Organizing the Unorganizable

An estimated 1.5 million to 3.5 million undocumented immigrants live in the United States (Hill 1985; Passel 1986).[1] Half of this population — predominantly from Mexico and Central American countries — is believed to reside in California and one-third in Los Angeles (Passel and Woodrow 1984; Soja, Morales, and Wolff 1983). They have been blamed for virtually every societal ill — from depleting the genetic pool to causing gridlock on Los Angeles's freeways, taking native workers' jobs, and impeding unionization. Four of these workers are Carmen Quiñones, Amalia Rodríguez, Miguel Marín, and Graciela Miranda.[2] Each entered the United States surreptitiously, eventually found work in the same factory, settled in Los Angeles, and, despite his or her undocumented status, became involved in a labor dispute. Their stories are but four of the thousands at the heart of the undocumented immigration debate and this book.

Carmen Quiñones arrived in Los Angeles for the first time in March 1976. She paid for the trip with money she received as compensation for her father's accidental death as a longshoreman in El Salvador. Planning to remain in the United States for only two years, she made the trip alone, leaving behind her mother and two daughters. The first leg of her trek was by bus to Tijuana with the first of three "coyotes."[3] A second coyote helped her cross the Mexican-U.S. border; a third drove her to a cousin's home in Los Angeles. Predictably, the two years Quiñones believed she would be away turned into three, then four. Five and a half years later she returned to her family.

During her absence one of her brothers had been murdered. "They say he was killed by a death squad," said Quiñones. "Their faces were covered. They probably thought he was a *guerrillero*. But he wasn't." A few months after she arrived in El Salvador, armed men wearing masks invaded her home again.

> Five men came to the house looking for my older brother and began spraying the house with bullets. We were all told to lie on the floor, face down, with our arms extended. My mother and a couple of aunts were there. My brother was in the airport at the time trying to track down a package. They never found him. I became very afraid and the next day began making arrangements to leave. Things had gotten very bad while I was away.

As the civil war in El Salvador escalated, Quiñones became one of thousands of Salvadorans to flee the violence. She returned to Los Angeles with her mother and daughters and, with the help of a friend from El Salvador, landed a job at Camagua, a waterbed factory in Los Angeles. Her father and one brother had been involved in unions in El Salvador, but she never took any interest in their work and they never talked to her about it, let alone about their union participation. She never imagined that within the year she would be embroiled in a labor dispute and supporting the unionization of the plant: "I had never gotten involved in anything like that before. I just do my work and don't bother anyone."

While we talked over a cup of coffee in her home in south central Los Angeles, with police sirens sounding in the distance on a Wednesday night, a rat scurried across the floor behind her. The years of neglect by the slumlord had invited the vermin. The walls of the immaculately clean apartment were adorned with pictures torn from magazines, in a vain attempt to hide the cracks and peeling paint. In the kitchen her daughters worked on their homework, seemingly oblivious to the tears that occasionally welled up in their mother's eyes. The tears were triggered as much by the thought of a future of virtually inescapable hardships as they were by the painful memories that Quiñones related to me. She spoke openly of her concerns about her daughters' education and the drugs and violence in the schools and neighborhood: "You work hard, overtime, sometimes you get home and the girls are asleep; you even work Saturdays and Sundays, but it's never enough to improve your situation. At least not very much."

Amalia Rodríguez, Quiñones' coworker and adversary during the organizing campaign, lived with her two children and a male companion in a cramped downtown Los Angeles hotel room. The kitchen was a hotplate. The bedroom was a mattress on the floor next to a bunkbed. She apologized for conditions but, alluding to the many homeless people I had passed on my way to the hotel, added, "At least we have a place to sleep." With the help of a "Czechoslovakian" with whom she had been corresponding in Los Angeles, Rodríguez and her children had entered the United States without documents. When she arrived in the United States, she married the man with whom she had been corresponding, but left when he became verbally and physically abusive: "I could put up with it, but I didn't want my children to."

Rodríguez wanted to build a house for her family in Zacatecas, Mexico, and the trip north seemed like the quickest route to fulfilling this dream. The house, she noted with a great deal of pride, was built, but she had changed her mind about returning. She had decided to stay in the United States, although during the interview she expressed doubts about staying much longer because of concerns about her children — especially her son:

One year I sent him to Mexico to study. Here, he gets up, leaves with his friend upstairs, and goes to who knows where, and when I go to work, they come back here. I talk to him and ask him how after everything we've gone through he's not responding. Education is the basis for everything. I don't want him to end up like me. I'm where I am because I lack the preparation. I think he listened to me because lately he's been going to school and his grades have gotten better. But if I stay, tomorrow it will be something else. If I'm going to have problems, better to have them in Mexico where my family is. Soon there will be problems with drugs, gangs, fourteen- and fifteen-year-old girls with chil-

dren. I don't want that for my children. Maybe if we moved out
of the city . . .

A tall woman, Rodríguez was described by several fellow workers
and supervisors as a "strong and determined" person. But she was
tired. She was tired of the long hours and the monotony. She was
tired of worrying about her children, and she missed her family in
Mexico.

Recalling her opposition to the union, Rodríguez said, "I didn't
think it was fair to attack someone who had just given me a job. I
figured I could get what I needed in a nice way. If I needed
something I would just go and ask. If I didn't get it, I just didn't
think it was right to attack him." In retrospect, she believed she
had done the right thing, but two years after the contract was
signed, she was disillusioned. She and others had taken the company's side, but the company, in their eyes, had not reciprocated by
giving them the preferential treatment to which they felt they were
entitled for their loyalty. Supervisors told her that the union contract, in effect, prevented the company from showing its apprecia-
tion. She did not accept the explanation. As the date of the negotiations for a new contract approached, Rodríguez was rethinking her
opposition to the union.

Miguel Marín, born in Chihuahua, Mexico, in 1948 and raised
on a ranchito, entered southern California in 1969 through Cañon
Zapata, the most heavily traveled route of entry for undocumented
immigrants along the Mexico-California border. Here, every day
in the late afternoon (as I was able to observe on a number of occasions, including once in the company of a border patrol agent),
hundreds of people begin to gather on one side of the canyon.
Vendors sell food, clothing ("including sneakers," as a Camagua
supervisor noted sardonically), and other paraphernalia to those
waiting for the cover of night to cross. On the top of the hills,
border patrol agents wait for the dangerous cat-and-mouse game
to begin.

At dusk, on one occasion, I observed a young man, no more than fifty yards away, yell at a border patrol agent, "Pinchi gringo! Viva México!" The agent accompanying me, formerly a missionary in Latin America for two years, responded in Spanish, with barely the hint of an accent, "If you like it so much, why don't you stay there?" The young man and his friends laughed. The repartee — at times good-natured and at other times mean-spirited — continued until it was silenced by the night. Only the helicopter hovering above and occasional voices amplified by a loudspeaker broke the silence. The only lights were the lights of border patrol jeeps moving rapidly across the hilly, bumpy terrain and the helicopter's floodlight.

Agents with special heat-sensitive binoculars scanned the area before them; others listened for movement picked up by ground sensors. "I can't blame them," an agent said to me; "I'd do the same thing. We'll catch some of them, but most of them will make it. I just hope no one gets hurt." There had been reports of people robbing the undocumented, several controversial shootings of immigrants by border patrol agents, and physical altercations between agents and immigrants. On several occasions, immigrants, fearing they would be separated from the rest of the group, had been killed by cars as they attempted to cross a highway. Signs on these thoroughfares now warn immigrants and drivers of the danger.

Marín made it the first time, and without a scratch. When he first arrived, he worked in a myriad of unrelated jobs. Eventually he became a sewer in the quilting industry. The road to Camagua had been a difficult one. Once he was fired for being repeatedly tardy; he had been attending to his wife, who was pregnant, ill, and in danger of losing their first child. This and other painful events in Marín's life eventually contributed to a nervous condition that kept him out of work periodically. But he was never without work for very long. A well-established network of quilters and mechanics helped him find work each time:

We know one another. We know who's working where. So and so is working at Ortho, Simmons. So and so is at such and such a place. When you leave, you call one of the mechanics that goes around fixing the machines and ask him where there is work. So when you go to a place, you know there's work there.

Sewing cushions is difficult work. Marín showed me his fingers, slightly deformed from the many years of pushing a large needle through heavy material that resists being poked. One of Camagua's most skilled workers, he had supported the unionization of the plant. But just as Rodríguez had become disillusioned with the company, Marín and several other workers became disenchanted with the union. He and some of his fellow workers wondered if they had not been sold out.

Graciela Miranda was born and raised in Mérida, Yucatán. Friends and family living in the United States exhorted her to get away from her husband, who was in jail for beating her and almost killing one of their sons. A very religious woman, she asked God for a sign. When she was able to obtain from acquaintances sizable loans for the trip, Miranda became convinced that this was the sign she had been awaiting. She, and later her children, traveled to the United States with tourist visas and, like so many other visitors, remained after the visa expired.

Miranda got a job in Camagua with the help of an old friend from Mérida, Fernando González, who was a supervisor at the plant. She had bumped into him accidently. "At first we didn't recognize each other. It had been a long time and both of us," she chuckled, "had gotten a little chubbier. We talked for hours about home." The reunion turned sour when he began to harass her sexually; he was the second supervisor to do so:

> Fernando threatened to fire me if I didn't go to bed with him. I was about to bring my kids at that time and he knew it. Before leaving Mexico, I heard about things that happened to people here, but I never imagined it would happen to me. I even had to fight him off. One day he drove me to a motel. I was offended. I

felt cheap. I told him he was mistaken. Normally I am cowardly and cry easily. But that day I got brave and told him that if I lost my job, I would take him with me by telling the company and his wife. He left me alone after that.

Miranda did not support the union: "I told the organizers that I was a Christian and could not be involved in those things." The fact that she was undocumented did not affect her decision: "I'm not afraid. I trust in God. 'Father, you've taken care of me this far; you'll keep taking care of me. And the day you want me to return to Mexico, you'll permit whatever to happen.' "

This book is about immigrant workers in Los Angeles who entered the country without documents, worked, raised families, and organized effectively to improve their conditions of work. In January 1985, Camagua's undocumented workers voted by more than a two-to-one margin for union representation and engaged in a successful fourteen-month struggle to secure a contract. How they were able to do this is the question — in its simplest and most fundamental form — that this book attempts to answer.

In large part, the answer emerges from conversations with the workers. Asking the workers themselves about the organizing campaign and their migration and work experiences allowed me to probe the issue of undocumented status as it shaped their lives and world views. The interviews were "conversations with a purpose" (Berg 1989:13). I wanted to reconstruct their world as *they* defined it. Common sense tells us that the fear of being apprehended and deported by the Immigration and Naturalization Service (INS) should make these workers virtually impossible to organize. The reality, as elucidated by these immigrants, is more complex and offers some hope to immigrant workers exploited by their employers and to a labor movement struggling to survive.

Organized labor in the United States is on the ropes, bruised and fighting back sporadically — and usually ineffectively. The crisis is reflected in statistics on union membership and other measures of organized labor's strength. Membership in unions declined from 35 percent to 17 percent of the total workforce between 1945 and 1985 (Adams 1985; Kokkelenberg and Sockell 1985). The Bureau of Labor Statistics reported on February 7, 1990, that 37 percent of all federal, state, and local government employees were unionized in 1989, compared to only 12 percent of private sector workers (*Daily Labor Report* 1990). Between 1980 and 1984, the work force increased by 4 million, yet unions lost 2.7 million members (Adams 1985:26). In the 1950s, unions were winning nearly 70 percent of representation elections; in the 1980s, they were enjoying only a 45 percent success rate (Galenson 1986:68). But this figure conceals the fact that collective bargaining agreements often are not reached. In the early eighties, approximately one-third of election victories by unions resulted in a contract (Cooke 1985b). Moreover, the amount and frequency of concessions to management in the seventies and eighties were unprecedented in U.S. labor history. While the AFL-CIO (1985:6) dismisses "prophecies of doom and despair," recalling that similar, unfulfilled prophecies were made in the 1920s and 1930s, there is little question that labor at the beginning of the 1990s is engaged in a difficult, uphill battle to recapture lost ground.

Among the explanations for labor's diminished strength, especially in some regions of the country, such as the Southwest, is the presence of undocumented workers.[4] Undocumented workers from Mexico and Central America are said to act as deterrents to unionization because of, first, their structural location in the labor market and, second, their legal status.

Undocumented workers are concentrated overwhelmingly in and their presence is said to help maintain the secondary labor market, a sector of the economy with relatively low levels of unionization (Briggs 1978, 1983; Fogel 1978).[5] The labor movement in this sector is "relatively underdeveloped," in part

because the social characteristics of the workforce, the multitude of firms in the particular industry, and the small-scale, lo-
calized nature of production obstruct the organization of strong
unions. Further, highly competitive product markets, rapid
business turnover, small profit margins make it costly for employers to recognize unions. (O'Connor 1973:14)

Peripheral industries tend to be small and labor intensive and offer
workers low wages, few advancement opportunities, and little job
security (Bluestone 1970:24; Piore 1975:126).[6] These factors, in
turn, are said to lead to short job tenures. In peripheral firms,
relationships between workers and supervisors also tend to be
"highly personalized" (and paternalistic), which "leaves wide lati-
tude for favoritism and is conducive to harsh and capricious work
discipline" (Piore 1975). In these respects, Camagua was typical of
secondary labor market establishments.

These conditions of course make the organization of *all* workers, not just the undocumented, more difficult, but not impossible.
Despite these formidable obstacles, unions, historically, have had
some success organizing workers in certain sectors of the secondary labor market. The concentration of undocumented workers in
the secondary labor market, however, does not explain the decline
in union membership, nor organized labor's poor showing overall
in this sector of the economy, especially since World War II.

The tendency to generalize from employment and unionization
trends in industries in which Mexican immigrants work, while
ignoring declining union strength in industries in which they do
not, should be avoided. Foreign competition, demographic shifts,
union policies and outlook, the activities of large corporations, and
the actions of governmental regulatory bodies have all played
important roles in the decline of the labor movement in the United
States (Mines and Kaufman 1985).

The second explanation for the unorganizability of undocumented workers is that undocumented immigrants' fear of ap-

prehension and deportation by the INS forces them to tolerate low wages, abusive treatment by supervisors, and otherwise poor working conditions, which citizen workers in these industries refuse to tolerate. Moreover, the argument continues, when these workers attempt to unionize, "the illegal Mexican aliens are frequently used as strikebreakers" (Briggs 1978:217). As one labor relations expert contends, a number of different characteristics, tied to "unlawful and alien status," make "the illegal an ideal worker for the secondary employer — one who will accept poor wages and working conditions and is unlikely to resist work speedups or insist upon complete equity of treatment by his employer" (Fogel 1978:110). Even more unequivocal is the following assertion: "As long as illegals are vulnerable to deportation they will be ultimately impossible to organize into viable unions" (Jenkins 1978:529–30).

The unorganizability of undocumented immigrants has been proclaimed as well by observers of industrial labor relations outside of academia and organized labor. The following assessment was proffered by the *Los Angeles Times* labor columnist Harry Bernstein (1985:1): "The millions of workers who are in this country illegally seldom join unions, and they almost never go on strike or otherwise complain about their wages or working conditions because they fear deportation and the return to the poverty in their homeland." The unorganizability of undocumented workers because of their legal status has become a "pseudofact," that is, a case "in which the fact itself has yet to be established" (Merton 1959:xiv–xvi). An example of this is the contention by J. F. Otero (1981:2), an AFL-CIO official, that "illegal aliens" are highly vulnerable and "obviously . . . represent a labor pool that is more docile . . . than the American workforce." My research calls into question this "fact."

Not only have undocumented workers in the secondary labor market participated in existing unions; in some cases they have contributed openly and militantly to organizing drives and contract negotiations.[7] This study challenges the conventional wisdom regarding the unorganizability of undocumented workers. Rather than viewing undocumented workers as beyond the pale of unionization, I suggest that their organizability depends less on citizenship status — which is singled out in most accounts — and more on labor market forces, the legal environment, organizational capacities, forms of labor control, migration and settlement patterns, and other such factors. In short, the elements that promote or retard unionization among the undocumented are not unlike those that determine the organizability of other workers who are similarly located in the labor market.

Instead of asking why undocumented workers rarely organize, I attempt to identify conditions under which they have organized. By posing the problem in this way, I hope to shed new light not only on the migratory and labor market experiences of undocumented workers but also on the nature of the crisis facing organized labor. This study also addresses the need for intensive studies on unapprehended undocumented immigrants.[8] Through a deviant case analysis of Camagua, a plant in which undocumented workers voted overwhelmingly for union representation and waged a protracted organizing campaign to obtain a collective bargaining agreement, I attempt to answer the question of why undocumented workers have organized despite the threat of apprehension and deportation.

A deviant case analysis is designed to identify elements that explain a theoretical deviation, in this case, a marginal, competitive firm in which virtually an entire work force of undocumented workers won a union contract, despite strong employer resistance. The objective is not to refute extant theories, but rather to refine and build on them. Neither is a deviant case analysis meant to imply that there is one and only one deviation. Lipset, Trow, and Coleman's (1956) classic deviant case analysis of the International Typographical Union (ITU) was not the sole exception to relevant theoretical expectations about union democracy, nor is the Camagua case the only one in which undocumented workers organized. The task is to select a case that deviates as much as possible in some theoretically significant way from that predicted by an established theory. The Camagua case satisfies this criterion.

This study, then, is a deviant case analysis of a plant in which 160 workers, virtually all of them undocumented immigrants from Mexico and Central America, voted by more than a two-to-one margin for union representation and negotiated a contract with their employer. At the time of the organizing campaign, Camagua produced foam and quilted products as well as waterbeds. I selected Camagua from among other companies because of the legal status of its workers and its location in the secondary labor market. Undocumented immigrants accounted for approximately 95 percent of the workers in Camagua and almost the entire leadership in the organizing campaign.[9]

Moreover, Camagua was typical of secondary labor market firms employing undocumented workers in Los Angeles County. In addition to the characteristics of secondary labor market firms listed earlier, establishments in this sector of the economy are characterized by strong employer opposition to unionization — and Hiram Ramírez, Camagua's founder and president, was not an exception. Employer resistance is an important factor, because typically it is isolated by researchers as a, if not *the*, major obstacle to the unionization of workers, regardless of citizenship status.

While the Camagua case does not invalidate the unorganizability thesis, it does highlight the need for greater "specification."[10] The following is a summary of my "amendments" to the conventional wisdom on the unorganizability of undocumented workers:[11]

First, few organizers fear anything more than fear itself among workers they are attempting to organize. The success of an organizing campaign rests heavily on the ability of workers to overcome their fear of reprisals. Perhaps no fear has a more paralyzing effect than that of losing one's job. Organizers in the Camagua campaign, as well as organizers from other unions, were unanimous on this point. As Jaime Montes, an organizer with over twenty years of experience in Los Angeles, remarked, "Like any other worker they're afraid of losing their job. That's what really worries them, not the 'migra.' "[12] Indeed, I was surprised by the relative absence of fear of apprehension and deportation by the INS among undocumented workers. Graciela Miranda's observation of the INS was fairly typical: "At no time was I ever afraid. I've only seen them on television."

As the four vignettes in the beginning of this chapter suggest, the fear of the INS had been mitigated by a number of factors. Miranda's comment touches on one — the invisibility of the INS in Los Angeles. As one of my colleagues remarked: "Out of sight, out of mind?" Another important factor is the settlement processes of undocumented immigrants. The trend in this century, which has accelerated in the past twenty years, has been toward "permanent settlement."[13] Length of stay, roots in Los Angeles, and family and friendship networks are positively related to the unionization of these workers. Marín's reference to the network of sewers and mechanics is illustrative.

Every worker I interviewed had family members or friends from home — either documented or undocumented — already residing in Los Angeles when they arrived. Even the majority of the Salvadorans interviewed, despite having arrived mostly after 1980, had fairly extensive family and friendship networks in place. Typical of the comments that underscored the importance of these ties was the following observation by a Mexican forklift driver, Tomás Colón. Affirming that he had come alone, Colón added,

> My two sisters were already here. One of them had been here for ten years. No, longer than that! Maybe eleven or twelve. I stayed with her for a while, but they were both married and they had their own families and all. So I moved in with a couple of guys from my town who had just arrived. It worked out really well, because if one of us was without work the others would help him out. Now I have my own family, but now and then a relative or

friends stay with us until they get a job and a place to live that they can afford. A couple of times entire families, kids and all, stayed with us.

In the Camagua case, family and friendship networks played a key role in the unionization of the plant — both directly and indirectly. Directly, these ties were used in the recruitment and commitment-building phases of the organization of the plant. Indirectly, they helped workers settle permanently and more comfortably in this new environment. This, in turn, made them easier to organize.

Perhaps one of the most striking examples of the positive effect the stability of immigrant communities has on unionization efforts is the successful grape boycott and organizing campaigns of the United Farm Workers (UFW) during the late sixties and early seventies. Many of the pickers lived and held a variety of jobs during the off-season in the Delano area, thereby facilitating the UFW's organizing efforts. The history of the unionization of immigrant workers in this century is checkered with other examples.

A related explanation for low levels of unionization in the secondary sector and the undocumented communities is short job tenures. Secondary sector workers are said to move from job to job too frequently to be organized easily. Undocumented workers, largely concentrated in the secondary sector, are believed to have even shorter job tenures — in part because they are believed to work for only a short time before returning home. But the shortness of job tenures in this sector of the economy, and of undocumented workers in particular, may be exaggerated. The tendency toward permanent settlement among undocumented immigrants has contributed to longer job tenures, as have other factors. Leonardo Barrera, a sewer in Camagua, noted that on more than one occasion he turned down higher paying jobs: "I don't like going from job to job. No one does. Also, Camagua was doing well. Why change jobs for a dollar more, have to learn to get along with new people and supervisors, and maybe a few months later get laid off because I'm new or the company goes down?"

Another important mitigating factor was the union's determination to organize these workers. This is in part, but not solely, a question of resources; innovative organizing strategies and the determination of unions to organize these workers are important variables as well. In the Camagua case, the union invested considerable human and other resources to organize the plant. As many as eight organizers were involved in the campaign. While some of the organizers worked exclusively on the Camagua campaign, others worked on two or three campaigns at the same time.

The commitment of some unions to organize the unorganized — regardless of their legal status, location in the labor market, and ethnicity — was a key factor in organizing immigrant workers in the Southwest between 1900 and 1940. In the 1930s, leftists in the labor movement attempted to organize (in some cases successfully) workers that the American Federation of Labor (AFL) had labeled as unorganizable (and had treated accordingly). Only when unions were militant in their efforts to organize farm workers and other difficult-to-organize workers were they successful, and even then not very often.

A related factor in the Camagua case was the union's deftness in dealing with immigration and legal issues, including the protections provided to the undocumented, both as immigrants and as workers. Organizers were able to allay the fears of many workers by assuring them that they were protected — and, technically, they were and have remained so — by the National Labor Relations Act (NLRA) against unfair labor practices by employers. In fact, the success of an organizing campaign revolves in part around the union's ability to get the undocumented to see themselves first, if not exclusively, as workers and not immigrants. (Ironically, this is something many unions were slow to realize and others have yet to recognize.) The importance of this factor is underscored by the resistance of employers to unionization.

That resistance and the determination of immigrant workers to unionize is a recurring theme. Prior to World War II, growers, mine owners, and other employers resisted the unionization of their work force with unbridled determination. Equally impressive were attempts by some immigrant workers to organize, despite the very real threat (especially in the first half of the century) of deportation, physical injury, even death. Employer resistance remains an important variable in the contemporary period, as does the determination of workers to organize.

The state's role in labor disputes has been and continues to be an important factor. It is critical in several ways. For example, by controlling — through passage and selective enforcement of immigration laws — the flow of immigrant workers into the country, the government has influenced the size and composition of the labor pool and, consequently, the bargaining power of workers. Local authorities — especially prior to World War II — repeatedly protected the interests of employers by disciplining the labor force, often through the use of state-sanctioned violence to suppress worker uprisings. Since the 1930s, however, the Norris-LaGuardia Act of 1932, the NLRA (Wagner Act) of 1935, and other labor laws provide many workers — including the undocumented — with protection that workers did not have prior to the 1930s. The lax enforcement of immigration laws has helped maintain a supply of undocumented labor, and the recognition of undocumented workers as "employees," under the NLRA, has facilitated their unionization. The supply of this labor is an important one for many employers in southern California, and this, in turn, has an impact on the organizability of these workers.

In the secondary sector of the economy, undocumented workers occupy a specialized occupational niche that provides them with a substantial measure of security and confidence. The demand for their labor is virtually indisputable. Undocumented workers are fully aware of this demand and of the cost to employers of high turnovers and interruptions of the production process. When I asked Fernando Alicea, a sewer in an innerspring mattress factory, whether he feared being fired, he responded, "Sure, but I also know I can get another job easily. There are places in Los Angeles that hire only people like me. Everywhere I've worked, everyone, or almost everyone, was illegal." Furthermore, if employers call the INS, they run the risk of becoming identified as employers of undocumented workers or the type of company that calls the "migra." By identifying themselves in this way, they compromise their ability to attract undocumented workers in the future.

At Camagua, the type of labor control employed by Ramírez and the inefficient transition from one type of control to another were also important factors in the unionization of the plant. The personal relationship between workers and their employer is an important variable, especially in small firms where simple control, or paternalism, is the mode of labor control. The breakdown of these ties in Camagua left workers feeling betrayed. It also undermined Ramírez's ability to use his personal ties with workers — many of whom he had known for years. This factor was tied inextricably to the poor and abusive treatment of workers by supervisors. Many of the workers referred to this deprecatory treatment as an issue of dignity. María Gómez, a mender and a Camagua employee for nearly ten years, remarked, "I know I don't have a lot of preparation, but I expect to be treated with respect. If you don't have dignity, what do you have?"

Bread-and-butter issues alone do not explain why workers organize and may in fact explain less than is generally presumed. The issue of dignity emerged time and time again in conversations with respondents and played an important part in the organization of the plant. María Gómez's comment is but one example of this. It was an issue that organizers recognized — and capitalized upon effectively.

The principal sources of data for this study were intensive interviews with forty-nine of Camagua's workers, four of the supervisors during the organizing campaign, Camagua's owner, the company's vice president for marketing, and the company's human

resources specialist, six of the eight union organizers, the coordinator of a corporate campaign waged by the union, and the union's
attorney. Additional interviews were conducted with twenty-two
workers who had participated in union organizing campaigns at
other plants, six members of management from other waterbed
and innerspring mattress manufacturing firms, seventeen union
organizers and business representatives from other unions with
considerable experience organizing undocumented workers in Los
Angeles County, four immigration and labor law attorneys, three
employees from two employment agencies, two INS officials and a
border patrol agent,[14] five representatives (including a Roman
Catholic priest) of organizations working with and serving as advocates for immigrants and Latin American refugees, and six aca-
demics with expertise in immigration and labor issues and knowledge of the history of immigrant workers in California and the
local area.

I also employed a semistructured questionnaire to collect data
on organizing campaigns (both successful and unsuccessful) at
other firms in which the vast majority of the workers were undocumented. I reviewed relevant primary and secondary written materials, including the union's files on the Camagua campaign and
several newspapers. The bulk of the data was collected between the
spring of 1986 and the summer of 1987 in Los Angeles.

Follow-up interviews, including discussions with respondents
about the collected data and analyses, were conducted through the
spring of 1988.[15] Interviews typically ran one and a half to two
hours, and in all but three instances respondents agreed to have the
conversation taped. Of the four telephone interviews that were not
taped, only one was conducted with an individual involved in the
Camagua campaign.

While I was able to establish the level of trust needed to get
workers to talk openly about their lives, I was surprised, nonetheless, by the lack of inhibition they exhibited in discussing their
citizenship status — especially on tape. No workers refused to reveal their citizenship status, and only a couple seemed at all un-

comfortable discussing it — and even then for only a very brief period. In fact, workers' willingness to discuss their undocumented status in a candid and relaxed manner, in a taped conversation, was an early indicator that perhaps citizenship status was not the deterrent to unionization that many had assumed.

Chapter II

The Organizing Campaign

Under certain conditions, immigrant workers, both documented and undocumented, attempt to organize. In some cases they do so successfully. The story of the Camagua organizing campaign provides the context for my analysis.

Camagua was founded in 1966 by Hiram Ramírez. Born in Puerto Rico, Ramírez migrated with his family to New York and began working in the bedding industry in 1948. According to a biographical sketch in a business magazine, "During the Depression era, it was not unusual for the young Hiram Ramirez to be awakened from a sound sleep at 6 in the morning to be told it was time to move. It was a strategy his grandmother employed to stay one step ahead of the landlord because she could not afford to pay rent" (*The Executive* 1987:84). In 1959, after working his way up from sweeping floors in a New York factory to managing a quilting plant in Minnesota, Ramírez placed an ad in a trade journal soliciting employment as a quilting plant manager. Minnesota winters had taken their toll. The following year he took a position as the business manager of a Los Angeles–based quilting company owned by one of the largest corporations in the bedding industry. After three years with the company, he inherited a small sum of money from his father and borrowed additional funds from family and friends. Then, Ramírez emphasized, he invested *his* own savings and refinanced *his* home to establish *his* own business. Within six months he broke even, and at the end of the year he showed a small profit.[1]

During the company's infancy, Ramírez, a quilter and mechanic, operated two quilting machines and a mending machine, answered his own telephone, wrapped rolls, and delivered them in his 1957 Ford Falcon — "two on the roof and two in the trunk." He fondly recalls leaving the phone off the hook during deliveries to give callers (and potential clients) the impression that he had a lot of business. In 1971, Ramírez added another product, fabricating foam for the company's own use and for sale to other manufacturers.

In the face of the increasing saturation of the quilting business and a recession in the early seventies, Ramírez turned his attention to waterbeds. Recognizing the growing popularity of waterbeds in the Southwest, he began experimenting with ways to solve some of the problems associated with the product. Ramírez collaborated with a producer of medical supplies and others to develop a new type of softside waterbed, for which he obtained a patent in 1977. The product catapulted the company to the top of the softside waterbed industry.

> Camagua's waveless mattress concept is based on the development of vinyl cylinders that are aligned side-by-side under a two-inch insulated quilted top, creating a sleeping surface with no hardspots or pressure points. . . . By varying the amount of water in each vinyl cylinder, each side of the bed can be adjusted separately to the desired firmness. Unlike the standard hardside waterbed, the cylinders prevent disturbing wave motions when moving, entering or leaving the bed. (*Camagua News*, undated, circa 1988)

Ramírez's rags-to-riches story is used by the marketing department in the company's sales strategy. According to a company press release, Ramírez's "success is the poignant portrait of a latter day Horatio Alger. A Puerto Rican, raised in the poverty of New York's Spanish Harlem, he was to demonstrate early-on Algerish qualities of pluck and industry." This background helps to explain Ramírez's dogged opposition to unionization. The perceived threat of unionization clearly was magnified by his humble beginnings and the fact that he had "sacrificed and risked virtually

everything" he owned to build a business "from scratch." An
abundant supply of low-priced workers in Los Angeles — many of
them immigrants — helped make it possible.

From the beginning, Ramírez employed undocumented immigrants, and on the eve of the union representation election in 1985,
roughly 95 percent of Camagua's workers were undocumented
immigrants from Mexico and Central America. Ramírez preferred
them over Mexican-American workers. "They were what we call
'pochos,' American born. But the illegal worked a lot harder."
Camagua certainly was not alone in employing undocumented
immigrants. According to several veteran organizers, citizen Latinos and undocumented workers from Mexico and Central America had become the preferred workforce in Los Angeles's bedding
and other secondary-sector industries perhaps from as early as the
mid-sixties.

In food, textiles, apparel, lumber and wood, and furniture and
fixtures, immigrants constitute from 55 percent to 90 percent of
the production workforce in Los Angeles County (Muller and
Espenshade 1985:58).

> Aside from the enormous size of the local market, one reason for
> Los Angeles's continued strength in manufacturing is its abil-
> ity to combine First World management, talent, and location
> with Third World labor, provided by recent arrivals from Latin
> America and Asia. Without this plentiful cheap labor Los An-
> geles would lose much of its garment and furniture manufactur-
> ing and distribution industries to lower-cost locations. (Lock-
> wood and Leinberger 1988:35)

The preference for these workers, expressed unequivocally by
Ramírez, was parroted by other bedding companies. On several
occasions, these expressions demonstrated strong racial biases
against black workers. One of the more blatant cases was revealed
by Arturo Madero, an employee of an agency that Camagua used
to recruit new or temporary workers: "Some employers tell us not
to send them blacks." Seeing the look of surprise on my face, he

added, "That's not that unusual. Other agencies will tell you the same thing." One other employment agency confirmed that, on occasion, they received similar requests, but they claimed, unconvincingly, that they did not honor them. Madero's employment agency acknowledged that they honored such requests.

Organizers were aware of these hiring practices. Michael Lutz, a business agent with a local union, recounted an incident in which they referred a worker to a furniture manufacturer. The employer called back, complaining that the worker, a Mexican, did not speak English. The organizer told him that the only other available worker with the skills they wanted was black. "Before I could finish the sentence, the guy said, 'Forget it; I'll keep this one.'" The incident, Lutz noted matter-of-factly, was a fairly common one.

While management representatives were more guarded in their comments on the subject, the president of an innerspring mattress manufacturing firm, William Greiland, who had arrived in Los Angeles after a long stint in Chicago's bedding industry, was quite candid — in part because he seemed not to understand fully the racist implications of his comments.

> In this market we're predominantly Hispanic. I don't mind telling you that I was somewhat disillusioned with the quality of work for us. We had some super good blacks [in Chicago]; don't get me wrong. But unfortunately they weren't a bunch; the percentage was not good. Here the predominantly Hispanic workforce I find it number one, very motivated. They go at it like hell! We got some super guys out there hand tying — very difficult work. . . . We taught every one of them their job, and they were eager and ready to learn. . . . If I were to give any given characteristic to the Hispanic worker that differs from the eastern black worker, I would say he's got a quality consciousness that's another three generations as far as they're concerned. It's an unhappy kind of a commentary, but that's a fact.

This company, among others, typically justified its preference for Latino over black workers on the basis of the Latinos' superior work ethic.[2] Soja, Morales, and Wolff's (1983:219) contention that Mexican and other third world immigrants — both documented and undocumented — provide Los Angeles with "perhaps the largest pool of cheap, manipulable, and easily dischargeable labor of any advanced capitalist city," is arguably more to the point in explaining the attractiveness of Mexican and Central American undocumented workers for employers. But while these workers tolerate wages and conditions that native workers — among them African-Americans — are less likely to endure quietly, their tolerance is far from boundless.

While many of Camagua's workers were dissatisfied with certain aspects of their employment, they had not considered collective action prior to 1982. A handful of workers complained on occasion, but most were reticent to do much more for fear of being fired. In this respect they did not differ very much from native, nonunion workers. One of the workers' principal grievances, in fact, was the capricious manner in which the power to fire was exercised by supervisors.

In the past, the owner's personal and paternalistic style had served to assuage many of the workers. Having endured economic hardships and performed menial work himself, Ramírez was able to relate to the workers and even served as a source of inspiration for some of them. Even if he failed to address their concerns in concrete ways, his accessibility and willingness to discuss their problems satisfied many of the workers, or at least served to dampen any emerging militancy. As Ramírez's company, his wealth, and the size of the work force grew, however, it became increasingly difficult for him to maintain the same level of personal contact and direct control. Furthermore, material class differences between him and his employees became more pronounced and obscured the shared experiences that in the past helped to maintain labor peace.

The impetus of Camagua's workers to rebel against authority was muffled by layers of conditioning and socialization. For example, many of the workers believed, as Amalia Rodríguez did, that if a man invested his money and built a company, he was entitled to run it as he wished. Rodríguez's earlier comment and the following observation by Juan Gómez, a warehouse worker, were typical: "It just isn't fair that somebody works as hard as he [Ramírez] did, and still does, and somebody comes along and tries to tell him how to do things. If they don't like the way he does it, they should leave and get their own business and run it the way they want to. It's *his* company!" The fact that Ramírez was a Latino, as they were, and that several of the workers themselves hoped one day to establish their own businesses, served only to reinforce this view for some. As Angel Versalles, a long-time Camagua employee, commented, "I know I don't want anyone telling me what to do when I have my own little business." Furthermore, for some of the workers, Ramírez had become a father figure, for others a kind of benefactor, to whom they were grateful for their job and livelihood. As Ozzie Alegría, a Versalles coworker in the warehouse and friend, said, "How can you turn on someone who gave you your job?" Felicia Gautier, also a long-time employee of the company and union supporter, noted that some workers actually referred to Ramírez as "Papi."

Organizing the plant entailed convincing workers that the employer's authority was not unbridled and that they were entitled to certain rights and protections as workers — irrespective of their citizenship status and personal relationship with Ramírez. The estrangement between the owner and his workers created by the rapid growth of the company and Ramírez's failure to anticipate the effects of this rapid growth facilitated the organizers' task. In 1973, the company's work force did not exceed twenty workers, but shortly thereafter Ramírez moved operations to a larger building and soon trebled the size of his workforce. According to Basilio Tirado — a supervisor who had been with the company almost from its inception, starting as a janitor in the late sixties — the size of the workforce "grew violently" after the invention and successful marketing of the new waterbed.

By 1984, the company employed more than 250 workers in four

separate buildings. Increasingly, Ramírez relied on a corps of supervisors, leadmen, managers, and vice-presidents to manage the
day-to-day operations of the plant. Their failure, especially that
of several supervisors and the owner's son, Bob Ramírez, to manage day-to-day operations effectively, opened the door just wide
enough for the union to slip in. A company front office employee
confided that Bob was too "rough around the edges." To illustrate,
he recounted the story of a three-way conference call between
Bob, Camagua's sales representative, and a prospective customer
in New Zealand. Bob asked the individual what the population of
his country was; when he responded three million, Bob laughed
and said that in Los Angeles alone they had eight million. Embarrassed, the sales representative interjected quickly that Bob "liked
to kid." On another occasion, Bob Ramírez asked a Mexican client
who Miguel de la Madrid, then the president of Mexico, was.
Néstor Rivas, the director of organizing at the time of the unionization campaign, observed that in the case of Camagua, as in so
many other campaigns, "The best organizer was the employer. We
just gave the workers the organization to go forward."

Efforts to unionize Camagua sputtered for two years. Gaspar
Amaro, a union organizer with the Clothing Workers Union
(CWU), first approached Camagua workers in 1982. Amaro himself had entered the country in 1972 from Nicaragua with a tourist
visa, but remained after it expired. Active in a teacher's union in
Nicaragua during the Somoza years, he worked in a number of
factory jobs in the United States before becoming an organizer for
the CWU. His first-hand experience as an undocumented immigrant and employee in factories similar to those he was trying to
organize were useful to him as an organizer.

The CWU had organized several quilting firms and, with the
help of a list of competitors provided by an owner whose firm they
had unionized, was seeking to organize other quilting establishments. According to several organizers, the practice is not unusual;
employers feel (and with reason) that they are at a disadvantage if
their competition is not unionized. As an employer (whose name

Amaro could not recall) put it rather graphically, "Now that you've fucked me over, here's a list of my competitors. Go screw them now." Ramírez's company was on the list.

Discouraged by the workers' initial indecision, despite clear evidence of widespread dissatisfaction, Amaro abandoned his efforts in Camagua temporarily. A second attempt by Amaro to organize the plant, as an organizer for another union, had to be scuttled when one of the two buildings in which the waterbed company was housed burned down almost completely.

> I left the CWU in November of 1982 and went to work for the United Furniture Workers' Union. I returned to Camagua with two others [organizers] and reestablished my contacts. We went to where they cashed their checks and got the telephone numbers and addresses of three of them. We asked them to come back the following week with other workers. This was January 1983. That Friday on our way there we saw a lot of smoke. I turned to Justino [another organizer in the car] and said, "I think that's Camagua." We couldn't get very close, but we were sure it was the factory. So we went somewhere else and basically forgot about it.

Amaro returned to the CWU and to Camagua in 1984 and reestablished contact with several of the workers. This time Enrique Bravo, one of the truck drivers he had met during an earlier visit to the plant, provided Amaro with critical information on the sites, the shifts, the hours, the nature of the work, and the workers. Far from spontaneous, the campaign required repeated home and plant visits and meetings. Networks played an important role, as workers recruited friends and family members. Virtually every worker interviewed found work at Camagua through a friend (or a friend of a friend) or a family member (or a friend of a family member). Also, as Amaro noted, "Salvadorans typically went after Salvadorans and Mexicans after Mexicans."

Despite only modest initial interest by workers to organize, an additional two organizers, Cecilia Durán and Juan Díaz, were as-

signed to the campaign. The three concentrated on one of the facil-
ities, visiting regularly, forming committees, and making home
visits. They had meetings Fridays outside of the factory where the
workers gathered to drink beer, to eat *ceviche*, or simply to socialize.
These contacts led to mildly increased attendance at weekly meetings in the union offices.

The process of identifying and securing the trust and commitment of discontented workers was a slow one, but the creation of a
company soccer team apparently accelerated the process. Amaro
claimed, however, that the soccer games did not bear heavily on
the success of the campaign, because the workers were too dis-
tracted (and in many instances too inebriated). "When you talk to
people, you have to have their attention. At the soccer game people are busy doing other things. If you held a meeting before practice, people would arrive late and others would be anxious to get
started. It wasn't a good way to get people." Three of the other
organizers, many of the workers, the owner, and several supervisors disagreed. For them, the soccer team had been an important
organizing vehicle. Ramírez was convinced that it was the soccer
team that triggered the organizing campaign:

> A bunch of guys wanted to start a soccer team, and I saw nothing
> wrong with that. I, in fact, encouraged it. We became a contrib-
> utor to it, but not a sponsor because of legal responsibilities.
> One day the captain of the soccer team asked Bob for some
> money. I think it was seventy or eighty dollars. He had one of
> these aggressions and said, "Fuck you guys" and whatever and
> that started it. Maybe it just took something to happen before
> these guys were triggered. I'm sure it was something that took
> place over a long period of time.

The owner even purchased the team's uniforms, prompting Basilio
Tirado to comment, "That's gratitude for you." Although no one
event triggered the campaign, the soccer games provided the organizers with the opportunity to speak with workers in a relaxed

setting and the workers with the chance to get to know the organizers on a more personal level. As Juan Díaz put it, "We identified with them, played with them. In an organizing campaign you need time and access. Tell them you're one of them."

Organizing Camagua posed special problems for the union because it was housed in four separate locations and each had two shifts.[3] For the most part, workers at different sites and on different shifts did not know one another. The soccer games and practices helped to bridge the gap, even though the players were principally from only two of the four locations. Workers played together, competed against other companies, and in the process developed a camaraderie that carried over into the organizing campaign.

The consumption of beer was an important ancillary activity at the soccer games, as it was on those Fridays when workers, after cashing their paychecks, gathered around a vending van to drink beer and eat seafood. Amaro recalled that it had been "a campaign of a lot of beer, a lot of liquor." Every Friday they would buy a sixpack, or twelvepack, or a case — "the women, as well as the men." There were occasions when the drinking made it difficult to have productive meetings. Juan Díaz recalled that "their drinking habits were a major issue. But you can't break their habits." Díaz added, however, that it made the workers more accessible and allowed the organizers to meet with groups of them at a time and gather information about the nature of the work, shifts, and grievances. In these settings workers discussed their grievances openly and found that they were shared by a much wider circle of colleagues than they first imagined.

While bread-and-butter issues were important in the campaign, as were complaints about increased production demands, the principal grievance aired by the workers was the abusive treatment by supervisors. Antonio Beltrán, an employee who worked on a machine that produced the material used to make the water cylinders for the bed, declared, "By allowing supervisors to be abusive, the company tells you it doesn't give a shit." Beatrix Pedroza, a mender, resented the lack of respect: "Even if you are not from this country and don't have legal papers or anything . . . that doesn't mean you're not worth the same as any person."

Supervisors often acted arbitrarily, reprimanding some workers and not others for the same infraction, and terminating workers for minor rule violations or simply because of personality conflicts. Male workers, in particular, reported having to endure humiliating public reprimands, often "in front of the women."

For the majority of the workers, Basilio Tirado and Bob Ramírez were the principal antagonists. Tirado conceded that he had made serious mistakes as a supervisor:[4]

> They come to work and one of their kids is sick and you're not understanding. That person then talks to others. When you hurt a person, it's like a cancer that becomes infectious. One person passes it on to the next, who passes it on to the next, and so on. When you make a mistake, it spreads and it's difficult to repair. It's lack of preparation.

Tirado acknowledged that he and other supervisors often behaved capriciously. "We may have been showing favoritism and that may have affected things . . . such as scolding some for coming in late and not others." Hiram Ramírez, in retrospect, wished that the supervisors had adopted his supervisory style: "You don't want these people to work under the fear of losing their jobs because one day you come in with an aggression and . . . they no longer have a job. . . . If you treat them with dignity, whoever it is, they're more productive. It matters how you feel about your work and who you're doing it for." On the other hand, Ramírez underestimated the connection between bread-and-butter concerns and the issue of dignity to which he referred. Being able to provide their families with the basic necessities and some luxuries is a source of dignity for workers as well. They resent deeply their inability to provide for their families adequately. As one worker, Raul Roldán, expressed it: "My wife has to work. In this country you can't make it if only one of you works. You both have to work. I wish I made enough so she wouldn't have to." Clearly embarrassed by the admission, he added, "Like they say, 'You have to swallow your pride.'" Several of the male workers were having difficulty dealing with disrupted or changing gender roles, such as the one described by Roldán. But they were slowly adjusting.

This is not to say that women and their relationships with their male coworkers and husbands or partners were unaffected. Both men and women reported strained relationships during the course of the campaign. In some instances, such as this one related to me by Laura Remondo, these strains clearly were caused or exacerbated by conflicting ideas of what constituted appropriate behavior for women:

> Fernando didn't like it that I worked. He wanted me home with the children. He had to cook and take care of them. When I got involved with the union, he got really upset because I was home even less because of meetings, and he didn't think it was right for a woman to be involved in something like that. I'm surprised he didn't leave me. I didn't do what he told me to do, and he even threatened to leave with the children.

Anthropologist Patricia Zavella's (1987) study of female cannery workers in the Santa Clara Valley revealed similar tensions.

At Camagua, increased production demands only aggravated an already deteriorating situation by increasing the pressure both on the workers and supervisors. In the building located on Packard Street, in particular, workers complained about the demands for more and faster production. An aggressive marketing strategy resulted in a dramatic rise in the number of retailers the company had to supply. To meet these manufacturing demands, without increasing labor costs appreciably, the company introduced an incentive or bonus system — or, as Ramírez preferred to think of it, he wanted "to compensate the high achievers." Taylorism, or scientific management, had arrived at Camagua.[5] For each task, an industrial engineer calculated the amount of production that a worker could reasonably perform within a certain time span. The minimum production expected was 85 percent of this calculated amount, and workers received bonuses for production above this level. While some of the workers welcomed the opportunity to increase their income, most of the workers interviewed, including those who supported the company, were not very receptive to the system.

Carmen Quiñones described the speed-up system instituted by the company to increase production:

> You're told you have to make five hundred, six hundred liners. Working without stopping. They have a camera on you, and a little box in front of you records each time the machine goes down [to seal the plastic liners]. They tell you what you are expected to produce in eight, nine, ten hours. I wasn't producing what I was supposed to. They have a chalkboard where they put up your name, and the ones who are producing what they want are in blue and those that don't are in red.

She paused and, with her voice cracking, added, "I have to go faster . . . kill myself." But even workers who were able to meet or surpass these minimal production demands complained of backaches, headaches, and high levels of anxiety.

Manuela Guindín, who had entered the country without documents or a coyote, was one of the company's most productive workers and one of the more vocal union supporters. She sewed the quilted tops, or panels, described in the company newsletter quoted earlier in the chapter. Guindín could produce as many as five or six hundred of the two-inch panels in an eight-hour day, and eight hundred of the one and a half inch panels. She explained her ability to easily surpass the company's expectations of 365 in the following manner: "It's my rhythm. I get tired if I'm working slowly. My body, my system is already accustomed to that rhythm. Like a machine." Sitting at her station with her Walkman strapped to her side and earplugs in place, working at a fast and steady pace, Guindín's machine analogy was a disturbingly appropriate one. Yet, after nineteen years with the company she was making just $6.90 an hour. She had reached her ceiling, prompting a fellow worker, Lourdes Acevedo, to observe that "there's a ceiling on wages, but not on production."

Both men and women experienced the aches and pains and most of the indignities. But some tribulations only the women endured. A couple of the organizers and several workers noted that women often were sexually harassed. Graciela Miranda's story was one of several in Camagua and other plants. A number of the workers in Camagua could not name even one supervisor, all of them male, who had not propositioned a female worker at one time or another. Felix Montero, a supervisor especially notorious for using his position — often indiscreetly — to demand and exact sexual favors, was fired by Ramírez for sexual harassment, according to several organizers and workers. Of the nineteen female production workers interviewed, nine reported having been pressured by supervisors — explicitly, implicitly, or both — to sleep with them. All of them knew of others who had been sexually harassed. In another plant, one supervisor was known to have a bed in a back room. As one worker commented wryly, "The bed was not there for occasional naps."

Female heads of households raising children by themselves were particularly vulnerable. The following remark by Justina Ríos, a Camagua employee, echoed the feelings of other women in this position: "When you're the only provider, you're in a difficult situation. I've been lucky. I haven't gotten fired for saying no, but my sister was fired from two different jobs for refusing to sleep with her supervisors. If you had a husband, maybe they'd respect you more or at least if you got fired, you could live on his income until you got another job. It's hard." In Camagua this engendered ill feelings toward the company on the part of several of the women and a few (though still some) of the men. As Fernando Núñez, a young man who had joined the company early in the organizing campaign, commented, "If Ramírez doesn't take care of you, if he doesn't get his supervisors to respect our women, what are we supposed to do? The union said they'd put a stop to it." Clearly, mistakes by Camagua's supervisors were pivotal in the campaign.

The supervisors' inability to supervise effectively can be at-

tributed partly to the sudden expansion of the company's operations and the owner's negligence in training them properly. The
transition from a small, marginally profitable operation to a larger,
more profitable one, was not smooth. Rivas summed it up succinctly. "What happened to this company was that it was a small
company and overnight became a large company. There was no
time to train supervisors. They would appoint anyone as supervisor. A company with 250 workers needed a better way to supervise its workers." But the issue was not one simply of poorly
trained supervisors. Many of the workers, and especially those who
had been with the company for at least four years, felt a sense of
betrayal or abandonment by the owner. The union offered them a
vehicle with which to translate their resentment into concerted
action.

In late October and early November of 1984, when workers'
interest in unionizing waned and the campaign failed to draw new
workers, Néstor Rivas, the director of organizing, began to reas-
sess the campaign. For four to five months the union had been
working with the same twenty to twenty-five men. By this time,
organizers had been assigned to all four sites. Amaro and Durán
were assigned to Packard Street, Rivas and Berta Moreno had the
Laredo Street site, Díaz and Celia Colón were organizing the
plant at Washington Boulevard, and Miguel Villareal and Nicolás
Gómez had the 183d Street site.[6] "Practically speaking," Amaro
noted, "there were four campaigns."

Discouraged with Camagua workers' response, the union notified the workers that because of waning interest in the campaign,
the next meeting would be the last. They were prepared to abandon the campaign, despite Amaro's insistence that the campaign
could be revitalized. He remembered being called "sentimental"
by his colleagues for wanting to persist with the campaign. His
assessment, however, proved to be correct. The union was surprised by the number of people in attendance and the new faces at
the next meeting. Even more encouraging was the fact that there
was now a much better cross section of the company's different

positions, departments, and shifts, and some key players were participating for the first time.

Javier Santiago, a mechanic and someone Amaro had identified as a "natural" leader early in the campaign, attended for the first time and immediately served as the spokesperson for the group. "In addition to being a mechanic who had contact with everyone," commented Amaro, "he had certain leadership qualities. When they went for beer, he'd put his money down first and the others would follow."

Elaborating on the importance of Santiago to the campaign, Amaro added,

> He had control over a lot of guys who took his lead. He had always been a leader. Everyone liked and respected him. Even Bob Ramírez liked and respected him. The others saw that he got along with Bob and figured if they followed him, they could get favors. What Javier said, they would do, because of his closeness to the company. If Javier said this wasn't good, let's organize, they'd do it without hesitating.

Ironically, many of the workers' respect for authority, in this case Hiram Ramírez's son, helped to legitimize Santiago's position. He was also one of the best educated workers in the plant.[7] But Santiago expressed little interest in the campaign when he was approached initially. He had hurt his leg badly and was in the process of buying a house with Lourdes Santiago, his wife, who also worked in Camagua as a sealing machine operator. When he joined the organizing campaign, following a couple of conversations with a fellow mechanic who had chosen to support the union, it was a tremendous boost for the union's efforts and lent a certain legitimacy to the campaign in the eyes of many of the workers.

Santiago was familiar with unions in Mexico and believed they were corrupt. When he arrived at the union offices for the meeting, he asked for assurances that this union was not corrupt and proposed asking a number of questions before he and others made up their minds. Rivas said that he responded by saying, "I don't know you. I've never seen you at a meeting. I have no problem answering you, but if I answer satisfactorily, you have to commit yourself to sacrificing your time and money and risking your job with the others. I'll answer all of your questions, and you in turn take on the responsibility." He agreed to Rivas's condition and the workers asked the organizers to leave the room.

Néstor Rivas was an extremely important player in the campaign. A native of Guadalajara, Mexico, he arrived in the United States in 1966 at the age of seventeen to join his mother, who was separated from his father. The son of a politically active electrical worker, Rivas said of his arrival in the United States, "When I came to the United States, I wanted to make money. I was not politically conscious. If there was an instinct, it was very hidden. I just wanted to make money." He worked initially as a busboy and dishwasher, eventually making his way to the garment industry, changing jobs frequently. In the early 1970s he became a supervisor in a garment shop, but was fired for advising and helping workers to organize. The CWU offered him a job, which he rejected initially because it paid much less than what he had been making. He later relented, accepted the job, and in 1982 became the union's director of organizers. As an organizer he was unrelenting in his efforts to organize immigrant workers. In the Camagua campaign he, more than any other organizer, commanded the admiration and respect of the workers and evoked the greatest ire (and respect) from Ramírez, his supervisors, and the workers opposed to the unionization of the plant. What he said and how he said it belied his sixth-grade education.

Because of Rivas, Marín, who, along with some others, wondered whether the union might have sold them out in the end, stopped short of saying so: "I have a lot of respect for Mr. Rivas. He's a fine person and the little guy (*chaparito*) is all man. It's only because of him and the respect I have for him that I could not say the same thing [that he sold them out]." Carmen Quiñones recalled that Rivas could "really talk," as could Amaro and another organizer whose name she could not remember. But "if Rivas wasn't there, sometimes people would not stick around. They came to listen to him. He speaks with authority. He raised your spirits."

When the organizers were asked to return, the workers had a list of questions waiting, which Santiago asked and Rivas answered. Rivas's recollection of a portion of the exchange was corroborated by several of the workers and other organizers present:

> "Could we be fired?" I said, "Of course." "What will the union do if they fire us?" I remember saying that the union would not do anything for you or anyone if you're fired. What are you going to do for yourself? How are we going to work together? First, we have to identify who is the union. If we're going to identify the union as this building or me, it's better that we don't do anything. You want to organize the company. What are you going to do for him or him for you if you're fired? What we can provide is a lawyer and the experience we have on how to minimize the risk. If there is a firing, to try to win it. That's all. "If we go out on strike, how much will the union give us?" Nothing. If we're going out on strike, we have to prepare early by raising money. The union doesn't have much money for that. It can help with maybe thirty dollars a week. They asked me who paid me and how much I made. I showed them a pay stub and said that the dues from 275,000 workers pays my salary. "How are you going to guarantee that you don't sell out?" They had to insure that some idiot like me didn't sell out. The best way was for them to take the reins of the campaign in their own hands. They wanted me to promise that they would get certain wages and benefits, but I said I couldn't promise it.

Durán had been hesitant to leave the room when Santiago asked them because she believed he was "with the company." She recalled Rivas convincing her to relax:

> Javier did all the talking for them. He started asking, but I don't recall them [the questions]. There were eight questions. Nestor

answered them one by one. He was beautiful. He answered each one. By the end of the meeting, Santiago said that next week they would have a meeting and to give them cards and they would bring them back. The following week we had about one hundred people. It was really Javier Santiago who they all looked up to.

Satisfied with Rivas's responses to their questions, the workers informed the union that they were prepared. Rivas responded that the union was not, unless they could get 90 percent of their fellow workers to sign authorization cards. The union was hoping for 70 percent. Rivas pointed out to the workers that they had been meeting with the same twenty workers for five months. Three weeks later, roughly 80 percent of the workers had signed authorization cards and the union immediately petitioned for a National Relations Labor Board (NLRB) election.

The union moved quickly, but was slow to incorporate the women in the plant into the campaign. The organizers allowed themselves to be swayed by male workers who contended that the women could not be trusted to be quiet in the early stages of the organizing drive when secrecy was demanded. As Manuel Laza, a sewer, put it, "As you know, women are more fragile, and the owner would have gotten wind of what was going on more quickly. But once we saw we had more support, we started bringing the women in." Male workers also questioned women's militancy and their ability to engage in a protracted and potentially rough campaign. Several organizers urged the male workers to incorporate the women earlier, but they resisted.

CWU organizers, and virtually every other organizer interviewed, knew from experience that these workers' beliefs about women as union activists were incorrect and unfounded. A number of organizers, both in the CWU and other unions, argued that women were more militant than the men in organizing campaigns. A couple qualified it by saying that it was more difficult to get women involved, especially women who were single heads of households, but once they were in, they were more committed and worked harder — despite, in most instances, having primary child-care responsibilities. One common explanation, or theory, for this was that women tended, as a rule, to commit to things more deeply than men. Typically, proponents of this view offered personal relationships, especially marriage (fidelity), as examples. Another explanation preferred by organizers was that women usually had responsibility for running the household, that is, for buying food, purchasing clothes and school supplies for the children, taking the children to the doctor, and paying the rent. As a consequence, a couple of organizers conjectured, women were most *directly* affected by low wages and poor medical and other benefits.

The women in Camagua who supported and worked for the unionization of the plant were but a recent chapter in a long history of union activism by Latinas in the United States. Among the first industries in Los Angeles to attract Mexican workers in large numbers was the garment industry. Mexican women predominated, constituting, for example, 75 percent of the workforce in dressmaking (Acuña 1988:221; Duron 1984:149). Despite the fear of deportation and an atmosphere of red-baiting and anti-unionism, Mexican garment workers struck in 1933 in Los Angeles. "The spirit of the strikers was excellent. The Mexican girls and women, who were by far the majority, acted almost like seasoned unionists" (Pesotta 1944:40).[8] Mexican women — both documented and undocumented — participated in agricultural strikes during the 1930s. In the cannery and pecan-shelling industries, as in the garment industry, they were in "the vanguard of the rank-and-file" (Acuña 1988:200). In 1939, over four hundred workers, mostly Mexican women, walked out of the California Sanitary Canning Company (Cal San) demanding higher wages, better working conditions, the recognition of their union, and a closed shop. "The Cal San strike marked the beginning of labor activism by Mexican cannery and packing workers in Los Angeles" (Ruiz 1990:264). In the Toltec Foods strike of 1975 in Richmond, California, 150 workers, most of them immigrant Mexican women, won a wage increase, improved working conditions, and better benefits (Mora 1981).

In the case of Camagua, once incorporated in the campaign, women played pivotal roles, although very few assumed (or were permitted to assume) significant positions of leadership in the movement. They did sit on the organizing and negotiating committees. In retrospect, Celia Colón, a popular organizer among Camagua's pro-union workers and someone who had worked in the garment industry when she arrived from her native Ecuador, believed very strongly that the union had made a mistake by not incorporating women earlier and in more significant ways: "We shouldn't have listened to them [male workers] the way we did. We knew better, and in fact the women showed how good they were once they got involved." Several male workers agreed with Colon's assessment. Among them was Rodolfo Romero, a Salvadoran with some union experience in his country: "I got strength from seeing the women involved. Why not me, a man?" After pausing briefly, Romero added, "It's also a little 'machismo' . . . to do things without being afraid." Other male workers acknowledged (albeit in a patronizing manner in some instances) their female counterparts' important contribution to the campaign. Several conceded that they were surprised. Some had mixed feelings about it. One of these was Jesús Durán, a forklift driver: "The women were just as loud as we were. Some of them even drank beer and hung out with us. I don't think it's proper behavior for a lady, but things are different here. You get accustomed to it."

Prior to the election, the union provided the company with a list of the workers on the organizing committee. This unusual tactic was one Rivas had employed in other campaigns to protect workers from being fired for union activities. When an individual files an unfair labor practice grievance with the NLRB, claiming that he or she was fired because of union activities, the employer can simply claim to have been unaware of the worker's support of the union. The list made it much more difficult for an employer to claim ignorance.

The company used what Rivas called the "vinegar and sugar" approach, talking to workers virtually every day, threatening and cajoling them. The company became aware of the unionization drive in the summer of 1984. Initially, management's response was to try to intimidate workers by observing (and glaring at) them when they spoke with organizers or by interrogating them concerning their and their fellow workers' activities. Tirado promised monetary and other incentives for information, and in fact paid one worker — Tomás Aguirre, a Guatemalan immigrant — for information on the union's activities. Concerned that he would be fired if he did not cooperate, the worker informed the union. The union told him to accept the proposition and to pass on useless and inaccurate information, which he did until the company realized that they were not getting their money's worth. Ramírez recognized that he needed outside help from people expert in preventing unionization.

Ramírez employed the services of a labor consultant and labor attorneys who specialized in helping companies prevent unionization. The labor consultant, Rafael Hernández, a former Teamster organizer, proved to be relatively ineffectual. He helped workers opposed to the union organize procompany rallies; he tried to discredit the union by citing past failures, including NLRB cases and instances in which the union did not provide members with adequate assistance; he warned workers that a union would result in stricter enforcement of work rules; and he misrepresented the cost of belonging to a union. He discredited unions based on his experiences as an organizer. Familiar with his style (and that of other labor consultants), the union prepared effectively to anticipate and minimize the effects of these tactics. The CWU, in fact, had a written profile of Hernández — as they did of other labor consultants used by employers to prevent unionization — in which his modus operandi was described.

The company fired a couple of workers prior to the election. On September 14, 1984, the union filed an unfair labor practice, charging that the company had discharged the two workers for engaging in union activity. The petition included charges that the company had committed an unfair labor practice by surveilling leafleting by workers and paying workers to spy on the union. The union charged that on August 8, 13, and 20, a supervisor had paid an informer for information. Tirado admitted to me that he had paid the worker and been tricked by the union.

Days prior to the election, the company circulated a memo among workers, reminding them that "no union could guarantee" wage increases, more benefits, and job security, adding, "You have no guarantee that the union can make good on the promises it has made. These are the facts, don't be fooled, vote 'NO' on January 11." The company's labor attorneys addressed workers as well, but made the mistake of asking supervisors and office personnel to translate for them. Union supporters, and many of the undecided workers, did not like these people. The messengers, not the message, were the issue for them.

The day before the election, the union, through friends of an organizer, received some airtime on a local Spanish-language radio station. A couple of the workers spoke on the air, and virtually everyone connected with Camagua listened to the broadcast. At the factory, pro-union workers cheered and released balloons. The idea, one worker explained, was to get everyone "thinking union." The company did not receive equal time.

The company's labor attorneys advised Ramírez to challenge the election, which the union won by a 113–48 vote on January 11, 1985. On January 18, the company filed an objection, charging that a non-Spanish-speaking NLRB agent "tainted the election atmosphere with partiality" by allowing and even requesting union observers to explain the voting process to voters. The union pointed out that during a preelection conference management did not protest when it was informed that the NLRB agent at one of the election sites was not bilingual. The company's attorney cited *Alco Iron and Metal Co.* (1984), in which new elections were ordered by the NLRB when one of their agents had a bilingual union observer explain voting procedures to Spanish-speaking employees. According to Camagua's attorney, the NLRB permitted known union supporters to monitor people waiting to vote, to electioneer illegally, and to coerce, both verbally and nonverbally, voters within the election area. This, the company argued, compromised the NLRB's neutrality and left the impression that the union and not the NLRB was responsible for running the election. The company also challenged the disqualification of approximately thirty leadmen from voting; the union claimed they were members of management because of their supervisory role.

The union saw the company's challenge of the elections as a delaying tactic and immediately charged the company with refusing to bargain in good faith. What the company wanted to do, the union charged, was to buy time and, in Amaro's words, "to demoralize the movement." Whether the company was delaying the process simply as a tactic to demoralize workers is debatable, but the delay did seem to have this effect in the long run.

The workers provided Ramírez with a petition signed by the vast majority of the work force, including many of those opposed to the union, asking him to drop the challenge and sit down to negotiate. The day that the petition was delivered to Ramírez, the majority of the workers on the day shift stopped work an hour early and attended a religious ceremony, or mass, held outside of the gates. Despite the petition, the walkout, and daily picketing by workers, Ramírez did not withdraw his appeal.

Since the number of votes contested by the company would not change the outcome of the election, a new election was not ordered by the NLRB in California. The company decided to appeal the election with the NLRB in Washington, D.C. In a letter dated September 11, 1985, from Ramírez to Rivas, the company advised the union of its intention to appeal and asked the union whether it would agree to another election on October 31, since appeals took so long to resolve. The union declined, and on November 7, 1985, the NLRB ruled in favor of the CWU. In the interim, numerous workers had been fired.

Beginning in February 1985, nearly one month after the election, the owner fired thirty workers for work slowdowns and fighting on the picket line. Two pro-union workers were fired on February 1, 1985, for allegedly threatening a supervisor, whom they claimed had threatened them and other union supporters. On February 12, a fight broke out between an independent trucking family and picketers, resulting in the termination of six workers. Armando Feliciano, a leadman, recalled, "Two of ours and two of theirs ended up in the hospital. It was a free-for-all, with sticks and metal pipes — everything."

On February 20, fifteen more workers in two departments were terminated for allegedly engaging in slowdowns. Organizers, in fact, told me that they had orchestrated the slowdown. The workers in question sat at two "round tables" sealing the plastic cylinders. Warned that production was dropping at an unacceptable rate, workers complained that the tempo was controlled by the leadpersons, both inexperienced. With the exception of one of the two leadpersons, all of the workers supported the unionization of the plant. The only individual in the two groups who was never warned, or fired, for lowering production was the leadman opposed to the unionization of the plant. The pro-union leadman was fired. José González, a worker at one of the tables, recalls asking why the other leadperson was not fired. There was no question that production had dropped appreciably, but production records were maintained by table and not individuals. The company claimed that they did not know who was or was not a union supporter, but two of them were members of the negotiating committee and the others all wore shirts, insignias, buttons, and other paraphernalia indicating support of the union. González's explanation for why the leadperson was not fired was simple and unequivocal: "Since he was one of their dogs, he wasn't fired."

The union filed unfair labor practice claims against Camagua in each case, charging that the workers had been fired unlawfully for engaging in labor activities. The union "won" only eight of the cases, although it was able to secure unemployment benefits for other workers. In the eight that the union settled with the company, the owner agreed to pay each worker six thousand dollars, the workers agreed not to seek reinstatement, and the union agreed to withdraw the NLRB charge. This was a settlement reached prior to the NLRB's disposition of the charge. The agreement did not preclude the union from seeking the workers' reinstatement in future contract negotiations. By signing the agreement, the company did not admit to any violation of the NLRA, but neither did the union nor the workers admit that the employer had acted legally.

In a memo to workers dated May 2, 1985, and beginning with "*Estimados Compañeros*," or "Dear Companions," Ramírez and his son Bob tried to correct what they claimed were false statements made by the union concerning the election, their appeal, and the termination of the workers. They accused the union of being interested only in collecting dues: "The union has been lying to you. The union is desperate and is disposed to sacrifice you, your job, your incomes and your family to avoid a second election. The union knows that by then you will realize that the only thing that they are interested in is your money." The company reminded workers that they had never disciplined anyone for simply supporting the union. They had fired workers for fighting on the picket line and lowering production. At the time, the dispute regarding the picketers had not been resolved, but the NLRB had ruled that the company had not violated the NLRA by firing the latter group of workers. They would not be reinstated or receive back wages.

The company also reminded workers that if they struck, to protest what the union called "illegal" terminations, they would not get their jobs back automatically, since the terminations had been ruled legal. The memo advised workers to continue working while the election challenge was being considered, assured them that the company would continue to operate with or without them, and warned them not to threaten fellow workers who wished to work. The memo ended with a telephone number for workers to call if they were afraid to work or had been threatened.

Ramírez was determined not to have his business unionized. He was convinced that unionization meant lower productivity:

> It's true that unions lower the productivity of workers. What happens is that the fastest worker works as fast as the slowest. The slowest sets the pace. With unions it's even more so. A guy comes in and wants to impress his boss. He works in a work crew where each is supposed to produce 100 pieces a day and the new guy produces 120. What do you think the others are going to tell him? To slow down. That's the effect unions have on the workforce. I'm not antilabor. I'm antiunion. There's a difference, I want you to understand. And it has destroyed this country completely.

The other company management officials interviewed did not share Ramírez's opinion that unions lowered production. Recent research on the subject, in fact, suggests that productivity is generally higher in unionized firms.[9] Ramírez based his opinion in substantial part on his own experiences as a production worker in New York, where on several occasions he claims to have been asked by other workers and union representatives to slow down. Conceding that once there had been a need for unions, Ramírez firmly believed that this was no longer the case. Today, he contended, employers treat their workers better and, in any event, there are laws to protect workers. He cited the decline in membership rolls as proof of the growing obsolescence of unions.

The success of his enterprise permitted him to resist as strongly as he did, perhaps spending more than one million dollars to fight the union. But it was precisely in this prosperity that workers wanted to share. While acknowledging the transgressions of some of his supervisors and his son, Ramírez believed that he was a fair employer and undeserving of the treatment that he received from the union and workers. Furthermore, he had worked too hard and sacrificed too much to allow a union to tell him how to run *his* business:

In essence, the union helps you run your company to their satisfaction. They don't have any stake in this. The employees gave them the right to do this. That's sort of unfair. I put up all of the money I had, I refinanced my house, I worked plenty of hours trying to get where I am, and then to come along and the union to say—who knows nothing about my business, by the way, and who knows nothing about running a business—to come in and say, "Hey, we're your partners; we're going to help you run the business."

The claim that unions reduce managers' flexibility is a common one, but, "all told, reductions in flexibility, while irritating to management, have only modest effects on productivity" (Freeman and Medoff 1984:172–73).

Ramírez deeply resented the personal attacks by the union and the effigies of him burned by workers. His response was not simply that of an entrepreneur, but of an individual protecting his name and reputation—a reputation he believed he had worked very hard to establish. Rivas shared with me recollections of a mealtime meeting requested by Ramírez, who wanted to express these very sentiments and to ask Rivas to stop the personal attacks. Ramírez believed that he was a decent man and good employer who cared about his workers. Rivas did not agree. As the campaign and conflict evolved, and especially after the union's election victory, the workers' and organizers' persistence and the owner's resistance became highly personalized.

Henry Beltrán, a seasoned Los Angeles organizer and president of one of the more active unions organizing immigrant workers, questioned the sagacity of personalizing a labor conflict to the degree that the CWU did in this instance. Such personalizing, Beltrán insisted, tends to complicate negotiations unnecessarily. He recalled instances from his lengthy career as an organizer in which employers and workers acted against their own self-interests because of personality conflicts and personal attacks.

Miguel Villareal, who became a CWU business agent after the Camagua campaign, pointed out that the company has never stopped trying to discredit the union: "We hurt Ramírez personally, and he'll never forget it." He believes, however, that in the Camagua case they had no choice but to go after him personally: "We couldn't get him to negotiate. Going after him personally was a last resort."

Before and after the election, the union tried, almost always successfully, to anticipate the company's next move. It obtained, for example, an antiunion video used by labor consultants and showed it to the workers, responding to each point contained in the video. The effect of this and similar tactics made the union appear more competent to the workers.[10]

The union employed several in-plant tactics to pressure the owner to negotiate. One tactic was to have entire departments call in sick on a given day. Workers came to work wearing T-shirts and buttons threatening to strike if they did not receive a contract. Other tactics included silent prayer and moments of silence, when the workers would put tape or a black-and-red kerchief over their mouths. On at least one occasion, a tape recorder played the following prayer: "This moment of silence is a chance for me to reflect upon this struggle I am engaged in; to show the company my discontent at their actions; to help me identify with my fellow workers; and to demonstrate to those who would abuse us that I am willing and ready to sacrifice for this cause."[11] Although the prayer was designed to strengthen worker unity, religion did not appear to play a prominent role in the campaign. Only five workers even cited their religious beliefs as a factor in their decision to support or not to support the union in the Camagua or other campaigns.

The company accused pro-union workers of trying to intimidate antiunion workers and committing acts of sabotage on the machines and product. While attempts by union supporters to intimidate fellow workers were not widespread, there is little question that some attempts at intimidation did take place. One union representative conceded that perhaps some of the workers "may have crossed the line" by smashing car windshields and flattening tires in the company parking lot, but added, "In any event, sometimes you have to lean on people a little bit." Although these tactics and minor acts of sabotage on the equipment (and perhaps the waterbeds themselves) served to harass the owner and his supporters among the workers, the most effective instrument used by the union to pressure the company to negotiate was a corporate campaign that included a boycott of Camagua's waterbeds. A full-scale strike had been ruled out by Rivas.

Rivas believed that a strike would not be effective. This was a belief shared by many other organizers operating in the same or similar industries in Los Angeles. In retrospect, however, some workers and organizers questioned whether the decision not to strike had been the correct one. Díaz believed they should have gone out on strike after the religious ceremony held in the parking lot: "But we hesitated. Workers were ready to go out. Instead we decided to slow down." Rivas maintains that strikes — while effective at an earlier time and still, perhaps, in some primary sector industries and firms — are not effective in the marginal industries in which the CWU was organizing (and not necessarily only in the case of undocumented workers). Workers are too easily replaced. And the laws, and the manner in which they are enforced, favor the employer.

Workers in Camagua, Rivas was convinced, were not sufficiently politicized and would have crossed the picket line. He conceded that on the day of the religious ceremony they might have gotten 65 to 70 percent of the workers to strike, but for only one or two weeks. Without the money to keep them out, they would have lost them. They also could have been replaced, and in four to six weeks the company would have been back to full production. Colón concurred, noting that during a two-day walkout following the suspension of Miguel Marín on April 30, 1985, many workers returned to work the second day and the company, which was

already recruiting workers from an employment agency, temporarily replaced the workers who were out. (Colón talked to the
people in the employment agency, but to no avail.)

Marín had been suspended for threatening another worker. Two
days later, 60 to 70 percent of the workers walked out, demanding
that he be reinstated. On the second day of the walkout, however,
the sewers reached a settlement with the owner and informed the
union that they would be returning to work. The sewers did not
consult the union or the organizing committee. Colón believed
that the problem was largely the union's own creation by according
special treatment to the sewers and other skilled workers. The
union had been courting them because they were the most skilled
of the work force and thereby the most difficult for the company to
replace. The special treatment the sewers received and the prima
donna manner in which they sometimes acted, Colón contended,
led to feelings of resentment on the part of some of the other
workers and ate away at the workers' solidarity.

Rivas believed that a combination of different tactics, or "tactical innovations" (McAdam 1983), would be more effective than a
strike. He knew that he had the votes to win an election, "but it's
much different to ask people to walk off and risk losing their jobs.
Votes don't mean that you have them." Rivas explained that it was
relatively easy to get workers to sign a card, but it was another
matter to keep and motivate them: "What is at stake with a strike is
food on the table, rent, and car payments. There are always some
prepared to strike, but the trick is to keep them out." Furthermore,
the only strike funds that the CWU had were thirty dollars a week
per worker. Instead of trying to stop production through a strike,
the union opted to slow down production by attempting to hurt
the company's sales with a corporate campaign and boycott of
Camagua waterbeds.

The corporate campaign, especially the boycott, required a concerted and sustained commitment by a significant portion of the
workers, at a time that some of them were becoming increasingly
demoralized. "The key challenge confronting insurgents . . . is to

devise some way to overcome the basic powerlessness that has confined them to a position of institutionalized political impotence. The solution to this problem is preeminently tactical." Insurgents must resort to "noninstitutionalized tactics" to take the struggle outside of "established arenas within which the latter derive so much of their power" (McAdam 1983:735). This is precisely what Rivas meant when he argued that the laws and the manner in which they are enforced favor the employer. They had to compensate and to do so created "negative inducements" (McAdam 1982, 1983) to force the owner to bargain in good faith. While the union and workers also used institutional means to obtain a contract (the election, participating in the collective bargaining process, filing unfair labor practices with the NLRB), it was the corporate campaign that proved decisive.

The union did not treat the campaign simply as a labor dispute. Organizers took advantage of every opportunity, and created some of their own, to present the Camagua workers' organizing efforts as a David and Goliath struggle. On the one hand, there was the successful businessman in his Mercedes Benz, and on the other, a group of poor immigrants simply trying to make a living and demanding that they be treated with respect. The union mailed over four hundred letters to organizations, including many unions, to make its case and to solicit their support of the boycott and other activities. The campaign generated letters addressed to Ramírez, urging him to negotiate in good faith. A former mayor and councilman of a neighboring municipality wrote to him on September 10, 1985, "I strongly recommend, as one Hispanic to another, that you recognize the right of your employees to organize a union. . . . I only hope that your success did not come about by stepping on people and at a 'win at any cost' attitude." The union also urged the mayor of Los Angeles, who had appointed Ramírez to a city commission, to pressure him to negotiate. In a letter dated February 28, 1985, the mayor responded that he had been advised not to become involved until the company's appeal of the election was settled. The owner was active in city politics and as such provided an inviting target to the union. But it was the boycott that provided the most critical negative inducement for the company to sit at the bargaining table and negotiate a contract.

The boycott was launched on April 23, 1985. Within a two-month period some two hundred stores stopped selling Camagua's waterbeds. The union employed Michael Kersey, an organizer who at the time was enrolled in an MBA program, to conduct research on the waterbed industry and to coordinate the boycott and corporate campaign on both the local and national levels.[12] The union observed that the boycott was especially effective in relatively affluent white areas, where, ironically, the racism of store managers and their patrons served to strengthen the boycott. Store owners and managers simply did not want a group of "dirty Mexicans," in the words of one retailer, picketing in front of their stores. In some instances, store owners called the police, but as long as the workers did not block the entrance or sidewalks, there was little they could do. Consequently, in white suburban communities, like San Clemente and San Miguel, many stores chose to discontinue the sale of Camagua waterbeds early in the boycott.

The nucleus of the boycott was formed by workers who had been fired by the company. Some of them remained active from the day they were fired to the day the contract was signed. The ties that developed between the workers and between them and a couple of the organizers were the strongest and most enduring. Durán remembered them fondly:

> Those are the ones I call my strikers. The ones I lived with. The ones Rivas would tell us to go to these stores where you have to take the bed out—we would take the bed out! That's what a boycott is. They were mine. We were a team. When one of them had something wrong, we all felt it. To think of those days . . . I love it. . . . I love those people.

On the way to boycott one store, Colón recalls telling the men in the van that they were twenty miles from the San Clemente border patrol checkpoint. They all began to scream and beg her to turn back. "We laughed a lot together," she said.

Kersey, the boycott coordinator, noted that they had mounted a successful campaign with only thirty workers. In some instances, deliveries were late because truck drivers were hesitant to cross the picket line. "Walters [the owner of a store picketed by the union], who purchases products from the company, said Smith Transportation Co., which is union affiliated, brings her the supply of waterbeds. She said orders have already come late because drivers will not cross picket lines at Camagua" (Lehto 1985:A2). The decision by L&M Furniture (a large chain of approximately seventy-five stores) to discontinue sales of Camagua's waterbed was a tremendous shot in the arm for the campaign and a setback for Ramírez. On weekends as many as forty workers and supporters from churches and other organizations picketed in front of some of the targeted stores. When Ramírez succeeded in getting a court order to reduce the number of picketers at the plants' gates, the union simply augmented the groups working on the boycott. The union also sent approximately forty workers to picket at the annual waterbed convention in Las Vegas, which Ramírez was attending with other members of management.

The boycott was intended to pressure the owner to drop the company's appeal of the election and negotiate a contract. The company responded by insisting that the election had not been a fair one. " 'If the union prevails in a fair re-run election,' " argued Gary Matthews, one of the company's attorneys, " 'the company will attempt an agreement in good faith. However, it will not be intimidated by illegal union tactics.' " He added that the boycott was an " 'act of desperation' " by a union trying to regain worker support (Lehto 1985:A2). Ramírez expressed concern to me that the union was hiring picketers and that some of them were violent and were attempting "to agitate the situation."

The owner, a vice-president, and a couple of supervisors conceded that they felt the effects of the boycott. Tirado noted that their warehouses started to fill up. Ramírez, however, denied that his decision to negotiate a contract was a consequence of the boycott. The company agreed to begin negotiations on December 23, 1985, after its final appeal in Washington, D.C., was

rejected by the NLRB in November 1985. By the time his appeals
of the election results were exhausted, active support for the union
had dropped appreciably. It was at this point that the owner made
his final, take-it-or-leave-it offer. The union and negotiating committee, concerned with the waning support of many of the workers, urged the membership to accept the contract.

While I was unable to obtain the actual figures on the extent of
the financial damage of the boycott, it was almost certainly a key
factor in bringing the employer to the table. The boycott had been
critical in the eyes of the union and its supporters — and, as noted,
even company officials conceded that Camagua "had felt" the
boycott (a confession tantamount to conceding that the boycott
had been effective). Typically, company officials downplayed the
impact of virtually every tactic employed by the disaffected workers, but with little prodding they acknowledged that by the fall the
boycott was beginning to hurt them. Furthermore, Ramírez remained combative during most of the boycott and the litany of
personal public attacks by the union, but he began to tire of the bad
publicity generated by the boycott in social and political circles
important to him. More important, he wanted to end the disrup-
tion of his business. Having lost the appeal in Washington, D.C.,
and fairly certain that the union would continue to boycott and
again file charges with the NLRB accusing him of bargaining in
bad faith, the owner opted to negotiate. The weakened position of
the union and negotiating committee permitted him to offer a
relatively diluted contract. Both parties thus attempted to maxi-
mize their outcomes by settling at this juncture.

The level of politicization, which Rivas gave as a reason for not
calling a strike, contributed to a weak contract as well. With
the exception of a half dozen union activists, none of the workers
had been involved in any political activity, let alone in a unionization drive. Despite attempts by the union to prepare them for a
protracted struggle, workers became frustrated and disillusioned
when they did not see better results quickly. As Amaro recalled,
"We had to keep motivating them. As incentives we used money,

food, and beer. We kept reminding them that had been wronged and that they had rights." As Tom McCartney, the CWU's attorney, pointed out, "The employer is negotiating for labor peace, so the more difficulties you create for him, the more incentive they have to settle. . . . The employer will give what he has to give, nothing more. Employers usually know what's going on on the shop floor. They have informants and other ways of determining union support." There had always been a small politicized and militant nucleus, but the support of their workmates deteriorated rapidly, and management knew it. Time tends to be on the side of the employer and Ramírez used it to full effect, on the advice of his attorneys, by appealing the elections and delaying the process.[13]

Despite attempts by the union to impress upon workers that they—the workers—were the union, many of them, if not the majority, continued to believe that the union had the power to secure for them a contract, irrespective of their own participation. Armando Amaral, a pro-union worker from Peru and one of the better educated of the workers in Camagua, recalled that there was substantial support for the union initially, but

> without [the workers] doing a great deal. They thought it was enough just to say they wanted a union. That's where the problems began [after the election]. . . . Though I had little experience with unions, I knew that things you wanted wouldn't just fall out of the sky for you. You had to struggle for them. But the workers didn't see it that way.

In Peru, Amaral had worked in a large, British-owned textile manufacturing firm as a quality control inspector. There he observed and grew to respect what he believed was a strong union. He recalled that when workers stopped, *every worker* stopped: "Not here. That was the difference." Not an uncommon dilemma for unions. In this case, the problem was aggravated, and expectations raised, by forms workers filled out in which the union asked them to list how much they made, the benefits they had, and what they wished to receive with a new contract. Many of the workers were disappointed with the union when it failed to deliver what they had written down.

The organizers conceded that the contract was relatively weak, but it was one that they had to accept because too much support had been lost and the possible alternative was no contract. Ramírez claimed, "The union won; we won; the employees lost. They collect their dues, and we won because they can't strike." But this was wishful thinking, for the workers clearly had been empowered. The contract, for example, protected pro-union activists, because Rivas was convinced that without a contract they would have been fired.

The new contract also offered a medical plan with no deductible, but several workers complained that with the old plan they had more options and shorter waiting periods to see a physician. For many of them, however, the five hundred dollar family deductible in the old plan made the inconvenience bearable. The wage increase was forty-five cents over a twenty-nine-month period (March 1986–October 1988), the life of the contract.[14] The major achievements were improved job security, a grievance procedure, access to legal assistance, and a growing sense of self-efficacy on the part of those who participated in the struggle to organize Camagua.

Despite the relative weakness of the agreement, which is not unusual for a first contract, especially in this sector of the economy, Camagua was unusual in that a collective bargaining agreement was reached fourteen months after the election.[15] This fact cannot be ignored in light of the claim that undocumented workers are unorganizable.

An interesting and unexpected outcome of the organizing campaign was the alienating effect it had on strong opponents of unionization. One worker, for example, Genoveva Vásquez, had worked for Ramírez for fifteen years and was among the leaders of the procompany faction. She, as did Amalia Rodríguez, expected to be rewarded for her loyalty, but became disillusioned when she was not. As Tirado observed, "She's not the same." When he explained to her that all of the workers were covered by the union umbrella and that, consequently, they could not give preferential treatment to anyone, she, Rodríguez, and several others felt betrayed. In 1988, they were considering supporting the union in the negotiation of a new contract, and were in fact present at a couple of meetings held to mobilize support for the new contract when the first one expired.

The undocumented status of the majority of the workers did not serve as a deterrent to unionization. The fear of losing jobs, not the fear of being apprehended and deported by the "migra," was their principal concern. Workers would make comments such as, "Let them call the 'migra' on me. In a week I'll be right back." Another worker believed it was not to the employer's advantage to call the INS, "because he would have been left without any workers. The only ones documented were his office workers." This was the case both for pro-union and procompany workers. But even the fear of losing their jobs was not sufficiently compelling to prevent many of them from organizing.

To allay any potential fears about their immigration status, the union assured workers of their rights as workers and provided information on immigration very early in the organizing campaign. The union also provided legal assistance in the event of an unfair labor practice by the employer or a raid by the INS. In the latter case, the prospects of a raid were practically nil, since the INS had a policy of not intervening in labor disputes. In the event of an unfair labor practice by an employer, Camagua's workers, despite their undocumented status, were protected by the country's labor laws.

Camagua workers thus joined the ranks of immigrant workers, who, despite their undocumented status, location in the secondary labor market, and strong employer opposition, organized. This occurred in a climate in which unions were losing members and experiencing tremendous difficulties organizing new workers, even in primary sector firms.

Chapter III

The World of the Workers

The image of thousands of "illegal aliens" living in the shadows is blurred by undocumented workers who have voted — despite the threat of apprehension and deportation by the INS — for union representation and negotiated collective bargaining agreements with their employers. The Camagua experience suggests that the assertion that undocumented workers cannot be organized is too sweeping. Undocumented workers *can* be organized, and the factors that determine success are not unlike those that facilitate successful collective action among other disadvantaged groups. This was the case in Camagua.

To assert that the deterrent effect of undocumented status on unionization is overstated is not to deny the significance of citizenship status in immigrants' lives. Citizenship is "a communal status which, while socially constructed external to the labor process, has considerable consequences for the organization of work and wages" (Thomas 1982:108).

> The greater exploitation of immigrant workers . . . is not a consequence of their docility or compliance, but of their objective vulnerability. Such vulnerability is a direct result of having crossed a political border. . . . It is the political status of immigrants and the legal relationship it entails with the state, which accounts for their objective position of weakness vis-a-vis their employers. (Portes 1978:474)

Undocumented workers are more vulnerable than native workers because of their legal status. As a result, within the secondary labor market, they occupy the most marginal and peripheral positions. But cheap labor is not necessarily docile labor. Many of the

Camagua workers' progenitors in the fields and mines of the Southwest demonstrated this earlier in the twentieth century, under conditions that were in most cases more onerous both for workers and unions.

In 1903, Mexican lemon pickers and graders in Santa Barbara won some concessions from the Johnston Fruit Company (Acuña 1988:155), as did Mexican and Japanese workers in Oxnard from the Western Agricultural Contracting Company (Arroyo 1981:6–7; Jamieson 1976:53–54). In 1917, 1919, and 1920, respectively, cantaloupe workers, citrus workers, and cotton pickers struck in different parts of California. In 1928, with the help of the Mexican consul in Caléxico, La Unión de Trabajadores del Valle Imperial (Imperial Valley Workers Union), a local of a newly created confederation, La Confederación de Uniones Obreras Mexicanas (CUOM—Confederation of Mexican Workers' Unions), led a strike against cantaloupe growers in Imperial Valley. Pea pickers in Monterey County and cotton pickers in Merced County also struck in spontaneous and unorganized actions in 1928 (Jamieson 1976:77). These strikes—precursors to larger, more frequent, and better organized agricultural strikes in the 1930s—did not escape the notice of Gov. C. C. Young's Mexican Fact-Finding Committee in 1930. "That the Mexican immigrants are beginning to orient themselves in California is evidenced by the fact that they have begun to organize into unions for the purpose of improving living and working conditions in the land of their adoption" (*Mexicans in California* 1930:123).[1]

Between 1930 and 1939, more than 180 strikes occurred on California farms (Maciel 1981a:25). While it is impossible to pinpoint exactly the extent of their participation, most of the strikers were Mexican (Gómez-Quiñones 1970:121). State, city, and county authorities typically backed the employers; strike leaders often were arrested; strikebreakers were brought in; and striking workers were terrorized by vigilantes. These factors and the union's meager resources all contributed to more defeats than victories for farm workers. Employers used deportations, and the threat of deportation, effectively; but these tactics failed in many instances to have the dampening effect on worker protest that employers and local authorities desired and expected.

The experience of both entering and living in southern California illegally varies among immigrants and over time. The effects of undocumented status on the lives of immigrants hinge on a number of factors. But the tendency has been to treat the threat of apprehension and deportation by the INS as a constant, that is, as if the experience of living and working in the United States without documents is the same for each and every immigrant and category of immigrants. The fear of the INS and the effect of that purported fear on undocumented immigrants' receptivity to unionization has been presumed and, therefore, not treated appropriately as an empirical question. The meaning of undocumented status for immigrants is conditioned by a variety of factors.

First, the fear of deportation by immigrants in Los Angeles is dissipated by the concentration of the government's efforts to control undocumented immigration along the border rather than in the interior. Second, undocumented workers fill a specialized occupational niche in the Los Angeles economy, which sufficiently emboldens immigrants to consider collective action when the conditions of work become unacceptable to them. Third, permanent versus temporary settlement may be a more useful distinction than documented versus undocumented status with reference to the organizability of Mexican and Central American immigrant workers. The social networks in which immigrants are enmeshed and which are strengthened over time facilitate the unionization of these workers, as do the longer job tenures of immigrants with plans to remain in Los Angeles.

Fourth, the form of labor control employed by a firm is an important factor. In the case of Camagua, the breakdown of the owner's paternalistic relationship with his workers contributed to the unionization of the plant. Fifth, the degree to which this segment of the workforce can be unionized rests substantively on organized labor's willingness, and capacity, to invest the necessary resources to organize it. Finally, Camagua's workers were considered employees under the National Labor Relations Act and thereby protected against unfair labor practices by their employer. This fact and the legal aid provided by the union emboldened these workers to challenge their employer. The message on a sign carried by an undocumented worker picketing a plant in 1978 said it well, "We may not have papers, but we have rights."

Camagua's undocumented workers' fear of the "migra" did not make them more difficult to organize than native workers or immigrant workers with papers employed in the same industries. Workers reported giving little thought to their citizenship status and the possibility of an INS raid of the plant. Eugenio Nazario, a forklift driver at Camagua, claimed that he had never been afraid of the INS, adding, "I've never seen them here. Only in Tijuana." And as Graciela Miranda commented in one of the opening vignettes in Chapter I, the only time she saw the "migra" was once or twice on television. Juan Maldonado, a worker in Camagua's vinyl cylinders department, said that he had a better chance of "getting hit by a car" — and he didn't worry about either. These views, while perhaps surprising, reflect both the subjective and objective reality of Camagua's workers and arguably that of a significant portion of the larger undocumented immigrant community in southern California.

Camagua workers' feelings of security rested considerably on the critical distinction between the threat of deportation and the actual enforcement.

> Whether deliberate or not, the impact of immigration laws and INS activities has not been to eliminate illegal workers but simply to maintain the formal threat of apprehension and deportation. Sustaining this threat, largely independent of its actual enforcement, is essential to the operation of the illegal worker system. (Jenkins 1978:528)

This distinction is pivotal for an understanding of the union activity of undocumented workers. Workers in Camagua clearly were not paralyzed by the threat of deportation.

Do factory raids, as Jenkins (1978) argues, "maintain the formal threat of apprehension and deportation" and, thereby, preclude the organization of undocumented workers into "viable unions?" While raids, and especially well-publicized sweeps, inject a dose of fear into immigrant communities, the fear appears to dissipate quickly — especially among long-term residents. The raids and INS personnel are too few, the employers and immigrants too many, and the penalties for both the employer and worker too mild for the impact to be very great. The probability of being apprehended in and deported from Los Angeles is minuscule, and returning, if deported, while not risk-free, is far from being an insurmountable task, especially for someone who has crossed the border previously.

The INS is not a highly visible force in Los Angeles, despite the image created by occasional newspaper articles on factory raids. "Apprehension efforts have not been focused on the central location for apprehending illegals — the place of employment. Instead, apprehension efforts have been centered along the border, leaving those who get past the border zone free to take whatever jobs they can find" (Jenkins 1978:527). In fact, a number of Camagua's workers had been caught — in some cases more than once — trying to cross the border surreptitiously, yet exhibited little concern once they made it to Los Angeles. I spoke with Gregorio Limas, a worker who cut foam at the time of the Camagua union campaign:

LIMAS: I felt relaxed when I arrived in Los Angeles.

HLD: As soon as you got here?

LIMAS: No, not right away! I mean, it takes you a little while to calm down. You don't know the city or anything. But you don't see the "migra" and there are so many others in the same situation as you. Nobody seemed worried. [Laughing] It took me a couple of times, but I made it.

None of Camagua's workers knew anyone apprehended in a factory raid and very few were acquainted with someone picked up by the INS in Los Angeles — and in at least one of these instances, the individual, with the assistance of an immigration attorney from a community service organization, avoided deportation.

Thomas Smith, a special assistant to the region's INS director, and Donald Keough, a coordinator of INS raids (or surveys, as the INS benignly calls raids) in Los Angeles, both acknowledged that detection and apprehension were much less likely to occur in the interior than at the border. Noting that there are probably "one million employers" in Los Angeles, Smith conceded that, "the chance of being surveyed or raided is very, very small." This assertion is supported by apprehension and deportation statistics. In 1984, for example, the year the Camagua organizing campaign was launched, 11,642 aliens were deported or "required to deport" by the Los Angeles district office of the INS. That same year the Chula Vista border patrol sector alone deported 407,828 aliens (*Statistical Yearbook* 1984:194–95). Clearly, the more formidable obstacle is getting into the United States; once in, the threat and the fear of being apprehended diminish markedly.

But even being picked up by the "migra" is not the specter generally assumed. As Limas explained, in a matter-of-fact manner, "It's natural. You expect them to send you back. After all, I'm here illegally; it's not my country. And if they send me back, I'll return." In response to the prospect of deportation, Camagua's workers responded that if deported they would have simply returned (in some cases, "after a short vacation"). Julia Real, a sewer, commented, "They're not going to kill you! The worse thing they [the INS] can do is to send me home, and I'll come back." In response to the surprise I expressed about undocumented workers' apparent lack of fear of the INS in Los Angeles, INS's Smith said,

> You're right — from the stuff you read in the papers you should be surprised, but if you think about it, you really shouldn't be, for this reason. If you have somebody who just comes across the border and is here, say, for up to four months, then the level of fear would likely be somewhat high, for a couple reasons. One has to do with the action of police forces in other nations, some

of which act extraordinarily brutally. So they don't really know, if we apprehend them, what's going to happen to them. They're not sure if it's not the same as back in their old country, and that sometimes means broken heads and cattle prods and all sorts of really terrible stuff. All that isn't true [of the border patrol or INS], but that doesn't matter, because if they think it is, it creates fear. In fact, the border patrol . . . except when dealing with smugglers or dealing with someone dealing with drugs, with those two exceptions — most people we apprehend, when you tell them to stop, you say "alto," and they do. You may have thirty or forty people and one border patrol agent says stop, and thirty of them stop. Why? Because they don't know if he's like some other policeman who might shoot. I'm glad . . . I mean, we really couldn't survive if we didn't have that reaction. A second reason is that people who become acclimated in one way or another, they get to know the factory routine; they get to know that a lot of people passing through don't have anything to do with the border patrol or INS. They get to know that a lot of people are in the same situation as they are. They get to know that they've survived. They may even get to talk to people who were apprehended and learn that while it was unpleasant, it wasn't brutal. And they stay here day after day and, you know, after a few months nothing has happened, and they've worked every day. So they begin to say, it could happen, but . . . obviously so many days have passed and nothing has happened.

Workers rarely mentioned the dangers involved in crossing the border and, even less, concerns about being harmed by the border patrol or INS agents. But "Americas Watch," an international human rights group, released a report on May 31, 1992, charging that the U.S. border patrol had been engaging in systematic abuses of undocumented immigrants along the Mexican-U.S. border (Rotella 1992:A3). The report, challenged by an INS official in Washington, D.C., came as no surprise to some groups that had been charging the border patrol with human rights abuses for many years. However, a couple of cemetery workers, Alejandro Berríos and Fernando Herencia, said that if they had a choice between being arrested by the border patrol or by the Mexican police, they would choose the former.[2] In immigrants' accounts of their entry into and their first few months in the United States, the fear of the unknown was a recurring theme. But it was a fear that time and experience allayed.

Interviewees related stories of people who were deported and were back to work soon after. Following a major sweep by the INS in 1982, a company's personnel manager told a *Los Angeles Times* reporter: " 'Some of them were here the very next day. They were deported that evening and they were back the next morning' " (Stammer and Valle 1982:16). Furthermore, as Special Assistant Smith confirmed, the INS has a policy of not intervening in labor disputes.

> SMITH: Each one [the employer or union] would call us to arrest the people who wouldn't vote for them. So one disadvantage was that we were upsetting the election. The second disadvantage is employers would call us shortly before a possible labor strike, and they would have us apprehend people. When we asked them if they owed them any wages, they'd say, "No." So we'd apprehend them and process them. Normally, though, if we apprehend somebody and wages are owed them . . . they collect those wages; then we apprehend them; then they go. But the employers, because of the bitterness of the impending strike will sometimes lie to us. It didn't happen sometimes. It happened frequently. So that was another reason we wanted to stay out of that situation. Because it was kinda unfair—it wasn't kinda, it *was* unfair.
>
> HLD: So it was an actual policy, not . . .
> SMITH: [Cutting me off] Yeah, it exists as a policy.

I told Smith of a labor dispute between management and largely undocumented workers in an electronics equipment factory where

INS vans arrived to find picketers in front of the plant chanting, singing, and carrying signs. They began to arrest people, but after being confronted by union organizers and a representative of management, the INS agent leading the raid placed a call to his supervisor. He was ordered to release the picketers and to leave the premises. Smith's assessment was that "in part, it was the bad publicity we would've gotten getting involved, but, the feeling was there are so many illegal aliens, why get yourself in a ticklish situation between forces when you don't have to."

Camagua's workers were informed by the union of the INS's policy not to intervene in labor disputes and they were reassured by it. In effect, state control was neutralized. This had not been the case when immigrant agricultural workers tried to organize prior to World War II. The intervention of the local police and immigration authorities on behalf of employers during this period significantly obstructed the unionization of these workers. Farmers' reliance on immigrant labor, however, tempered how often and in what manner local authorities intervened. In the 1928 strike against cantaloupe growers in the Imperial Valley, for example, the sheriff and district attorney threatened to turn over undocumented Mexican immigrants — the majority of this work force — to immigration authorities, but there is no evidence that any of them were actually deported (Wollenberg 1969:54). The demand for immigrant labor and employers' reluctance to involve immigration authorities persist, and in 1990 employers rely on the INS to discipline workers less than they did prior to World War II.

Organizers, labor lawyers, and community immigrant-rights activists noted that employers rarely call the INS, for fear of identifying themselves as employers of undocumented workers and hurting their recruitment efforts by becoming branded as an employer that calls the "migra." At least two employers acknowledged that these were actual considerations for them and for fellow entrepreneurs. One employer, Michael Reardon, remarked,

> I've never called the INS and can't see doing it. Whether someone is legal or not is not my problem. I'm not Immigration. As

long as others are hiring them, I have to hire them, and I don't want to do anything to make it harder to get them, like call Immigration. The word gets around, I'm told. I really don't want them [the INS] bothering me. We can take care of our own problems.

Neither workers nor employers appeared to be preoccupied with the threat of an INS raid, and this was reflected in the latter's hiring practices.

At Camagua, undocumented immigrants constituted virtually the entire production workforce, as they do in many other firms, suggesting that neither workers nor employers expect citizenship status to affect the normal conduct of business. Why would employers hire undocumented workers exclusively, or almost exclusively, if they felt that the probability of an INS raid was high? The INS does not differentiate between short- and long-term immigrants. Consequently, companies stand to lose "long-time, key personnel during INS raids, crippling their operations" (Mines and Kaufman 1985:224). Owners continue to hire these workers since the risk of losing them in a raid is minimal and the profits derived from employing them are substantial. Whatever reluctance organizers encountered in efforts to organize Camagua's workers was not due to workers' fear of an INS raid.

Organizers confirmed that workers rarely cited the fear of being picked up by immigration authorities as one of the, let alone *the*, principal reasons for not supporting unionization efforts. Workers' fear of losing their jobs, the most prevalent fear among all workers — undocumented and documented — is the most common obstacle organizers confront in their efforts. As David Ricardo, an organizer of food industry workers, observed,

They were scared that they'd lose their jobs. But we expect that, and while we can't guarantee that they won't be fired, we tell them that there are laws to protect them and that we will fight for them. But the fear of being fired is something definitely on their minds, especially at first. That's something anybody with a family has to worry about. You'd be crazy not to. But when the alternative is working for wages you can't feed a family with and being treated like shit, you get over it.

The fear of losing one's job is by no means an unfounded one.

Firing workers attempting to unionize is one way employers have historically resisted unionization, with varying degrees of success. Since 1960, it has been a common and effective tool for employers. Nationally, while the number of union elections remained virtually constant between 1960 and 1980, the number of charges involving the termination of a worker for union activity increased threefold (Freeman and Medoff 1984:232). Ninety-five percent of employer unfair labor practices result in some sort of employment loss (Cooke 1985a:437). In the Camagua case, nearly forty workers were terminated. Even when unions and workers receive a favorable wrongful-termination ruling from the NLRB, the effect on workers contemplating unionization is potentially chilling. But even the possibility of losing their jobs did not stop the majority of Camagua's workers from organizing. This was explained partly by their perception (supported in some measure by data on immigrant workers' labor market participation) that they occupy a certain occupational niche in the local economy.

The sense of security expressed by workers (and corroborated by organizers) lay considerably in their firm belief that native workers would not do the same work, under the same conditions, and for the same wage. Their lack of fear rested substantially in their unique position in Los Angeles's occupational structure and the demand for their labor in certain industries and jobs in the secondary labor market. As a garment worker commented to a *Los Angeles Times* reporter in the wake of an INS sweep, " 'They say these jobs belong to Americans. Lies! I have never worked in a place where any blacks or whites ever walked in the door. Only Latinos and a Chinese person here and there will kill themselves to work at these jobs. If they deport us all, they'll go naked' " (Becklund 1984:3). Félix Pavón, a worker in Camagua's foundation department, echoed the thinking of many of his fellow workers, when he commented that if the INS had come during the organizing campaign, "they would have had to take everyone!" As Lourdes Santiago recalled, "We thought they [INS] wouldn't [come] because there were a lot of people who supported him [Ramírez], and we knew they also did not have documents. They'd have to take them too." Camagua's employees were well aware of the fact that their coworkers were virtually all undocumented. Many of them had worked in other factories in which the majority of the workers were undocumented. As Rosa Mercado, a member in Camagua who had been in Los Angeles for nearly ten years and opposed the union, noted, "I've never worked anywhere where everyone wasn't illegal, and I've worked in about two or three places. I can't imagine '*gabachos*' doing what we do. The truth is that I've never seen them."[3]

Immigrant workers have become an important, if not an integral, part of the Los Angeles economy. "In terms of both sheer numbers and the historical persistence of this population movement . . . immigrant workers appear to play a more central role in the U.S. economy than any kind of a strict supplementary argument based upon the labor scarcities of an advanced industrial society would appear to allow" (Jenkins 1978:520). One researcher estimates that undocumented immigrants may make up as much as 81 percent of the work force in the Los Angeles garment industry and 75 percent in the restaurant industry (Maram 1980). " 'Without these people from south of the border, we wouldn't have an industry,' says Bernard Brown, the regional vice-president of a Levi Strauss unit that makes ladies' sportswear. 'It would be a catastrophe' " (Petzinger et al. 1985:1). In Houston, perhaps one-third of construction workers were undocumented, and in 1980 the INS even arrested eight undocumented immigrants working as landscapers at one of its own immigration-processing centers (Petzinger et al. 1985:1).

They not only fill a very large share of farmworker and laborer jobs; they also hold a major portion of the semi-skilled manufacturing jobs, and to a lesser extent, service and craft jobs. . . . In Los Angeles County, where 45 percent of the state's manufacturing jobs are located, Mexican immigrants fill a substantial share of all manufacturing jobs; they are also very important to the construction and personal service industries. (McCarthy and Burciaga Valdez 1985:17)

Furthermore, in many cases in which undocumented workers were apprehended by the INS, they were replaced by native workers for only short periods of time, only to be replaced, once more, by undocumented workers (Cornelius, Chávez, and Castro 1982).

In 1982, during the week of April 26–30, the INS picked up 5,635 "suspected illegal aliens" in nine cities nationally during their "Operation Jobs" sweep (Stammer and Valle 1982:1).[4] Unemployed native workers applied for the vacated jobs, but, as Alex Sytnyk, a personnel manager at B. P. John Furniture Company in Santa Ana said, many of them did not stay: " 'Some will accept it [the job] and as soon as they find out how hard the work is, they'll quit' " (Stammer 1982:1). By Friday of that week the Texas Employment Commission reported that it had referred only forty-two applicants for over one thousand positions once filled by apprehended immigrants in Houston (Tempest 1982:1). Eventually, many native workers showed up to inquire but left because of the low wages and poor working conditions. Tree trimmers, for example, made four dollars an hour cutting branches near telephone and high-voltage power lines. When these workers were informed of the nature of the work and the wage level, a commission employee said, " 'they told us to go to hell' " (Tempest 1982:1).

According to a *Los Angeles Times* survey of management, unions, and employees in Los Angeles and Orange counties, 80 percent (646 of 801) of the aliens apprehended during Operation Jobs were back on the job three months later. According to Stammer and Valle (1982:16), "Hal Takier, personnel manager of West American Rubber Co. in Orange County said, 'The Americans? None of them stayed, maybe 1 percent.' " In some cases, the return rate was nearly 100 percent. El Rey Mexican Foods reported that thirty-four of thirty-five apprehended immigrants eventually returned; at Acme Lighting and Manufacturing Company nineteen of twenty returned. (Stammer and Valle 1982:17). Even the police chief of Santa Ana declared on numerous occasions that INS raids were essentially ineffective in stemming the flow of undocumented immigrants into the area, noting that 99 percent of the undocumented immigrants picked up by the agency were back in the city within forty-eight hours. " 'We believe,' " Police Chief Raymond Davis remarked on one occasion, " 'that the INS would do best spending its time and money protecting the borders' " (Olivares 1983:2).

It is because of the "willingness" of the undocumented to endure low wages and poor working conditions in jobs that have become stigmatized and are unacceptable to most native workers that they occupy a particular niche in the economy.[5] In 1983, for example, poultry industry employers in Sonoma County could not find sufficient workers to replace immigrants who had gone out on strike. "No other workers in the area are willing to perform the arduous and dirty tasks involved in defeathering and preparing the birds for market" (Mines and Kaufman 1985:220).

While working conditions and the nature of the work at Camagua were not the most oppressive in Los Angeles, many of the jobs in the plant were repetitious and exacted a physical toll on workers. Some workers complained about having to stand all day, performing the same task repeatedly, and others expressed misgivings about the pace of the work—especially following the introduction of the incentive, or bonus, system designed to speed up production. While the sewers and several other workers earned between six and eight dollars an hour (and sometimes more with bonuses), new workers earned the minimum, and most of the workers, regardless of the length of their tenure with the company, hovered around the five-dollar mark. Camagua's workers were the most recent immigrants to perform the type of labor that immigrant workers had been performing for over a century in the United States.

Mexican immigrants, both documented and undocumented,

have been an important fixture in the economic landscape of southern California since the second half of the nineteenth century. With the Treaty of Guadalupe-Hidalgo (1848), ending the Mexican-American War, and the Gadsden Purchase (1853), the United States completed the conquest of over 918 million acres of sovereign Mexican territory.[6] In theory, the treaty extended citizenship to Mexican inhabitants choosing to remain in the newly acquired territory. Some Mexican citizens chose to leave, but the majority remained and became the first of many successive generations of workers of Mexican ancestry to serve as a source of cheap labor for employers in the United States.[7] The Mexican labor force which remained after the conquest, however, was insufficient to quench capital's thirst for cheap labor in the rapidly developing region of the southwest. "The Treaty of Guadalupe-Hidalgo . . . left the toilers on one side of the border, the capital and the best land on the other. This mistake migration undertook to correct" (Galarza 1964:14). By 1930, an estimated 1.5 million persons of Mexican descent lived in the United States (Bogardus 1934:16; Romo 1975:173). The vast majority toiled in the least desirable and lowest-paying jobs in the fields, mines, and railroads.

This massive migration is explained by a combination of factors. In Mexico, the Constitution of 1857 prohibited communally owned land. Although directed primarily at church estates, this law set the stage for the expropriation of land owned communally by peasants (Cockcroft 1986). With economic conditions in the central and southern regions of the country deteriorating in the second half of the nineteenth century, landless laborers headed to northern Mexico where the government had established a free-trade zone to attract settlers. The construction of railway lines connecting northern Mexico to the remainder of the country and the United States, encouraged northward migration from the interior in a number of ways. The railroad stimulated industries, contributed to the mining boom in northern Mexico, and "tapped the large pool of laborers in central Mexico" (Cardoso 1980:13). Harsh economic conditions and a volatile and dangerous political climate spawned by the Mexican Revolution of 1910–17 also served as a catalyst for northern migration (Reisler 1976). The foreign invasion of capital and the unequal economic and political relationship that developed between the United States and Mexico were at the turn of the century (and remain as we approach the end of the twentieth century) an essential part of any equation explaining the nature and persistence of undocumented immigration and immigrant labor in California. "The flow of Mexican migrant labor to the United States is a century-old phenomenon caused by Mexico's uneven economic development and vulnerability to domination by U.S. capital" (Bustamante and Cockcroft 1983:309).

On the U.S.-side of the border, the demand for labor, particularly cheap and flexible labor in the nascent agricultural, mining, and construction industries, and in railroads, increased dramatically in the early part of the twentieth century. The demand for agricultural workers was accelerated by large-scale irrigation projects created by the Newlands Reclamation Act of 1902, which turned thousands of acres of barren desert into some of the most productive land in the country; a climate that allowed for year-round farming; the invention of the refrigerated railroad car; improved canning and food preservation techniques; and the railroads, which linked southern California to the rest of the country and Mexico's interior (Reisler 1976). The activities of labor agents stimulated and facilitated Mexican immigration (Reisler 1974), but by 1920, "the internal migration of Mexicans to points at the border was self-sustained" (García y Griego 1983:51). Employers then concentrated their efforts on recruiting labor within the United States. The Chinese Exclusion Act of 1882 and other restrictive and xenophobic immigration legislation had all but eliminated Chinese labor, and the Gentleman's Agreement of 1907 and other legislative measures, including the Immigration Act of 1924, effectively put an end to Japanese immigration. Restrictionists — among them key figures in organized labor — were much less successful in stemming the flow of Mexican immigrants.

The Immigration Act of 1917 threatened to cut off the supply of

Mexican labor to the southwest, but agricultural, railroad, and mining interests managed to secure certain exemptions for Mexican immigrants. In May 1917, Secretary of Labor William B. Wilson waived the literacy test, head tax, and contract labor clause on a temporary basis for Mexican agricultural workers. Under continued pressure by agricultural and other interests, Wilson extended the period of admission and broadened the order to include other occupations (Reisler 1976:25–29).[8]

Wilson's suspension of immigration requirements were met by cries of protest from organized labor, but in the end it was the cries of the agricultural lobby that were answered. The temporary admissions program served as "a catalyst for augmented immigration. . . . As long as labor was needed in the Southwest, American authorities were quite lenient in issuing permanent immigration visas to Mexicans" (Reisler 1976:42). By the mid 1920s, "Mexicans had become a significant part of the nation's labor force, inhabiting the Midwest as well as the Southwest, and employed in industry as well as agriculture" (Reisler 1976:42).

The enormous contribution of Mexican workers to the development of the Southwest, particularly in agricultural, is indisputable. Orange production quadrupled and lemon production quintupled between 1900 and 1920. Between 1917 and 1922, the output of cantaloupe, grapes, and lettuce doubled, tripled, and quadrupled, respectively (Reisler 1976:5). By 1929, the Southwest was supplying 40 percent of the nation's vegetables, fruits, and truck crops. Mexican labor constituted 65 to 85 percent of the common labor used in the production of these crops (McWilliams 1968:85–86). Their contributions in the construction and maintenance of railways and a variety of other industries were equally impressive (Romo 1975:181).

The Immigration Act of 1924 failed to satisfy fully the desires of restrictionists to end immigration from Mexico, but it did make it more difficult for Mexicans to enter the country with a visa. The increased difficulty in securing a visa caused by a ten-dollar consular fee, a two-dollar medical exam, an eight-dollar head tax, and a literacy test as added requirements encouraged undocumented immigration (Reisler 1976:59; Samora 1971:35). To enter the United States without the proper immigration credentials was cheaper and less time consuming (Gamio 1971:10). In 1926 the California State Bureau of Labor Statistics estimated that 75 percent of Mexicans in California were undocumented (Daniel 1981:293).[9] "Distinctions between Mexican and Mexican American workers were not as hard as they are now. They were all Mexicans. Few were naturalized citizens of the United States" (Weber 1973:309).[10]

The Emergency Labor Program (Bracero Program) of 1942 (scheduled to end in 1953 but extended several times before it was terminated in 1964) was an attempt to control both the influx and placement of immigrant labor in the United States.[11] Instead, it may have stimulated undocumented immigration and movement into urban areas and nonagricultural work by immigrant workers. By the time the program ended, 4.6 million contracts had been issued to Mexican workers, or *braceros*, under the program (Garcia y Griego 1983:57). During this period, *braceros* established social networks in the United States and abandoned their jobs in the fields for higher paying and more secure, year-round manufacturing and service jobs. Many remained, or returned without documents, increasingly with families in tow, after their contracts expired. Employers wishing to avoid the red tape (as did many of the immigrants) and preferring workers more poorly protected than the *braceros*, increasingly employed undocumented immigrants. Employers in nonagricultural industries received them with open arms. Several of the workers I interviewed, both at Camagua and at other firms, had relatives (including some parents) who had been *braceros*.

The demand for and importance of Mexican labor in the Southwest did not diminish with time. In fact, since the late 1970s, this labor force has been augmented appreciably by immigrants from El Salvador, Guatemala, and other countries of Central America. Half of Camagua's work force was Mexican; the other half was made up principally of Central American immigrants, with Salvadorans constituting the majority of this group. Immigrant workers in Los Angeles are concentrated in nonagricultural sectors of the economy. According to 1980 census data on Mexican immigrants, one-third of males and two-fifths of females work in manufacturing, one-sixth of males and one-tenth of females in agriculture and mining, one-tenth of males in construction, and one-eighth of males in food retailing. Significant proportions of undocumented workers are also found in wholesaling and nonfood retailing, business and personal services (one-sixth of female undocumented workers), finance, and public administration (Passel 1986:193). Mexican and Central American immigrants in California share roughly the same market and occupational conditions (Wallace 1986).

The belief that Mexican immigrant labor was tractable, docile, and transient was as old and constant as the demand for their labor. For one thing, unlike African-Americans, Filipinos, and Puerto Ricans, Mexicans could be deported. Most often, however, the basis for this conclusion was biological or cultural. As one Texas farmer, cited by Robert Lipshultz (1962:5), said in the 1920s,

> The Mexicans are a wonderful people; they are docile; I just love them. I was paying Pancho and his whole family 60 cents a day before the war. There were no hours; he worked from sun to sun. . . . Don't get to pitying the Mexican and deprecating the white people, holding him in subjection. He wouldn't have it any other way. . . . The Mexican is a most honest man; and the damndest thief. But he figures, "I'm his, and so what is his is mine." It's just like the nigger, "Massa's nigger, Massa's watermelon," so it can't be stealing.

There were surprises in store, for both their transitory nature and their docility had been exaggerated.[12] Although the threat of apprehension and deportation did inhibit protest, many immigrant workers organized to improve their wages and working conditions.

This was the case in Camagua. While undocumented status certainly constrains the behavior and limits the options of immigrants, their feelings of occupational security mitigate the effects of their legal status. Their tolerance for low wages, poor working conditions, and abusive treatment is not boundless.

The century-old demand for their labor and the occupational niche they fill in Los Angeles's labor market have contributed to an increased tendency among undocumented immigrants to "settle" in Los Angeles.[13] Year-round work, particularly in the light-manufacturing sector, has led to longer-term employment and residency in Los Angeles. But during the first half of the twentieth century a process was put into motion, that took on a life of its own. Traditional, and popular, economic push and pull theories are inadequate to explain this migration and settlement process. Family reunification has become an important engine, and migrants' social networks have stabilized migration "by adapting to shifting economic conditions and by generating new opportunities apart from the original incentives" (Portes and Bach 1985:10). Stable communities are easier to organize. The length of time immigrants live and work in Los Angeles is inversely related to their fear of apprehension and deportation by immigration authorities. This was corroborated unequivocally by organizers, community activists serving immigrants, and the workers themselves.

According to one immigrant labor expert, undocumented workers are difficult to organize because of "the ephemeral commitment of some of them to their immediate jobs" (Fogel 1978:109). Typically, native workers shun low-wage, dead-end, and menial jobs; consequently, society has difficulty filling secondary jobs. Temporary migrants are one solution.

> Because they view their stay as temporary, they are undeterred by the lack of career prospects in the secondary labor market or by the short-run instability of the employment. Since they are only working temporarily and in any case derive their social

status from their roles in their home community, they are also untouched be [*sic*] the menial, even demeaning, character of the work. (Piore 1986:25)

But migrants sometimes change their minds.

The difficulty with temporary migrants as a solution to the problem of filling secondary jobs is that they do not remain temporary. While many, maybe even most, actually return home, a significant number end up staying longer than originally intended. They then tend to bring their families from home or to form new families, and as a result many of their children grow up in the country of destination. (Piore 1986:25)

In the past fifteen to twenty years there has been a trend toward more permanent settlement in the Southwest by undocumented workers (Cornelius, Chavez, and Castro 1982; Maram 1980; Massey 1985; Mines and Kaufman 1985; North and Houstoun 1976).[14]

Mexican migration clearly took a sharp upswing during the 1970s . . . and migration is a self-feeding process. Putting the two findings together, the logic is inescapable. The more people who begin migrating, the more people who will continue to migrate; the more people who continue migrating, the more who will inevitably settle in the United States. Thus any temporary migrant program or inflow of short-term undocumented migrants can reasonably be expected to lead to ultimate settlement in significant proportions. (Massey 1985:276)

Length of residency in the United States in turn translates into reduced fear of the "migra" and greater receptivity to unionization. This was the case, as well, with eastern and southern European immigrants in the early part of the twentieth century.

European immigrants with plans to return home typically tried to avoid anything that would keep them from their jobs for any extended period of time (Brody 1960). This included union organizers. Although eastern and southern European immigrants were more apt than their western and northern counterparts to return home, most of them remained — and it was they who were more likely to participate in union activities. "When the great mass of unskilled workers in the steel industry ultimately acted in the famous steel strike of 1919, it was primarily those immigrants who had their homes and families in this country who struck" (Rosenblum 1973:160).

The length of time residing and working continuously in the United States increases both the social networks and the information at migrants' disposable, which in turn affects their behavior in the labor market and workplace. "Although legal vulnerability undoubtedly influences the search for employment and the willingness to bargain for higher wages, the strength of this effect depends on the information available to the immigrant" (Bailey 1987:132). The more isolated a worker, the greater the effect of his or her legal status (Bailey 1987:133).[15] The probability of being recruited into a social movement is dependent mainly on "links to one or more movement members through a preexisting or emergent interpersonal tie" (Snow, Zurcher, and Ekland-Olson 1980:798).[16]

The social networks inside and outside the plant certainly facilitate the recruitment process. Employers use these networks to find new workers. This form of recruitment tends to raise the morale of employees, reduce turnover, and reinforce the paternalistic ties between the employer and workers. But these same ties can be used to organize immigrants. At Camagua, family members approached family members, individuals convinced their friends, and individuals approached other individuals performing the same or similar type of work. The successful recruitment of Javier Santiago, for example, was effected by a combination of appeals by a fellow mechanic and a family friend also employed in Camagua. As Amaro recalled, "I asked Raul León, a mechanic who worked with Javier Santiago, to talk to Javier and convince him to become active." When asked why León was recruited to talk with Santiago, Amaro responded,

Because they worked together and did the same kind of work. And they were making roughly the same money. Someone doing the same job or working in the same department is likely to be more influential than someone from a different department. If someone had approached Javier, once he moved on to his next job the conversation would end. Raul could stay with him and have a better chance of convincing him.

Organizers in Camagua, and their counterparts in other unions, utilized these networks whenever they could. Where they were nonexistent or weak, the task of organizing was encumbered.

The importance of these immigrant networks is found in other industries and regions of the country, including New York's garment industry.

> To be sure, home and job are not quite as glittering as the newcomer had imagined or the settler had promised, but importantly, the settler's neighborhood is home to other compatriots, and his job is one of many similar positions where other immigrants work. . . . Immigrants may be vulnerable and oppressed, but, because they can draw on connections of mutuality and support, they can also create resources that counteract the harshness of the environment they encounter. (Waldinger 1986:33)

Coyle, Hershatter, and Honig (1980) and Zavella (1987) document the importance of family and friendship networks in the lives of women workers in the El Paso, Texas, garment industry and the San Jose, California, canneries, respectively. These networks provided information on work-related problems, babysitting, and unemployment benefits, and served as a source of emotional support for their members. "In some instances, work-related networks became politicized after they were well established as social networks" (Zavella 1987:151).

Kin and work networks were important, as well, among cannery workers in the 1930s. "The UCAPAWA [United Cannery,

Agricultural, Packing, and Allied Workers of America] movement demonstrate[d] that Mexican women, given sufficient opportunity and encouragement, could exercise control over their work lives, and their family ties and exchanges on the line became the channels for unionization" (Ruiz 1990:272). In a number of attempts to organize Mexican immigrant workers, the importance of these networks and permanent settlements was evident even prior to the 1930s.

> Sufficient numbers had entered the United States during the previous decades to allow substantial numbers to root and settle into industries that required year-round employment. It was in those sectors of the economy that the pattern of resistance was the most intense. . . . Mexicans migrated to Los Angeles in great numbers and as the population settled, strike activity increased. (Acuña 1981:201)

While most migrants (perhaps two-thirds) were single men, by as early as 1910 "increasing numbers of men were crossing the border with families in tow, probably a sign that they were intending to stay in the United States" (Wollenberg 1975:101). Despite employer resistance, deportations, unwarranted arrests by the police, and the California Criminal Syndicalism Act (used to arrest and imprison Industrial Workers of the World and other organizers), "the steady growth and relative stability of a community of year-round workers contributed to unifying Mexicans." (Acuña 1981:211–13). Mexicans increasingly established themselves firmly in southwestern and midwestern rural and urban communities and formed mutualistas and other organizations that served as or facilitated the formation of labor organizations (Romo 1975:191). This tendency toward permanent settlement, while slow to unfold, picked up momentum after World War II and played an important part in the dissipation of workers' fear of the INS and their capacity to organize at Camagua.

Permanent settlement is generally accompanied by a change in frame of reference.[17] As immigrants become more integrated in the society, their perspective changes (Bailey 1987). Jobs, wages, and conditions they were once inclined (or felt forced) to accept, become less acceptable. "The shift from temporary migration to permanent settlement implies a fundamental change in perspective, which has repercussions in political and other forms of organizations" (Piore 1979:109). In their study of the social process of migration from Western Mexico, Massey et al. (1987:270) observed that "progressive integration implies a gradual shift in a migrant's focus of orientation from Mexico to the United States. In the early phases of migration, a migrant's primary frame of reference is the home community. . . . As they spend more time abroad, migrants pay increasing attention to their socioeconomic position in the United States."

With the passage of time, immigrants compare their situation less to what it was in Mexico or El Salvador, or what it continues to be for those who did not emigrate. They know how much money others like them are making. This phenomenon is not necessarily firm-specific. Workers' networks provide them with information on wages and working conditions in other Los Angeles firms. For permanent settlers particularly, this information is useful. The same phenomenon was observed earlier in the century with European immigrants.

> Recent immigrants generally did not have to meet the expenses of long-established American citizens: the cost of sending children to school, the property tax, the poll tax, the church donations, the insurance premiums, and the contributions to benefit societies. It was recognized that in the course of time the immigrant himself acquired many of these obligations and learned to demand higher wages. (Lane 1987:150)

Clearly, European immigrants at the turn of the century who did not have a family to support in the United States, required lower wages to live.

Trying to raise a family in Los Angeles with a low-skill, low-wage, dead-end job is a formidable task indeed. As María Fernández, an assembly worker in another factory, lamented,

> In the United States all you do is work. You get up early, go to work, work overtime, get home, and you're too exhausted to do anything but go to sleep, to get up again, and even work on Saturdays and Sundays. In Mexico we used to have time to relax and be with your friends and family. Not here. When my kids graduate from high school, I'm going back.

Commuter migrants from Mexico are willing to work for wages and under conditions "that are impossible for a person who must confront the daily cost of living in the United States on a permanent basis" (Briggs 1983:228). But what happens when the temporary migrant becomes a permanent settler or resident?

Reflecting on the effects of an immigrant's length of residency in the United States, Leandro León, with fifteen years' experience organizing immigrants in Los Angeles, observed,

> After working in a factory for six to eight months, he starts thinking of improving the work situation. He sees that he's barely making enough to live on and can't send money home. He can't have a comfortable and happy life that he wants. Even making minimum wage, he can rent an apartment with someone else, has a refrigerator, heat, kitchen and a rug . . . something he didn't have in El Salvador. But they organize because they see that they can do better here and increase the possibility of bringing his family. Here he begins talking to other workers and finds out that someone else is doing better. New comparisons begin, and organizing is seen more favorably.

Los Angeles is an expensive city in which to live. This immigrants quickly learn.

Not only do immigrants have to earn a wage that will allow them to feed and shelter their families; there are also the accompanying pressures of their children wanting what other children have and their own desire to live in a place, drive a car, and dress in a manner that symbolizes a certain level of success. As Frank Lauder, a union organizer, explained, "If his neighbor's kid has a Cabbage-Patch doll, then she [his daughter] wants one, and he wants to be able to get it for her." Margarita Méndez, a mender in Camagua, expressed it this way:

> He [the owner] drives a Mercedes and his son has a nice car too. They live in a beautiful home. What's wrong with wanting some of the same things? I don't expect ever to have what they have, but I think I deserve something better than what I have. I've worked hard, and I should have something to show for it. Don't you think?

As a rule, workers at Camagua, such as Rafi Catavino, a truck driver for the firm, compared their situations, almost exclusively, to other workers in Los Angeles — and not always to other immigrants.

> When I first got here, I thought I was doing well. Things were tight, but we had a roof over our heads — even though it leaked sometimes — and food. I even sent a little money home, though as the kids got older it was a lot harder to do that. In fact, sometimes I can't send anything for months. But I noticed that others just like me were doing better than I was, and they weren't working any harder. I paid taxes like everybody else. So why not try to progress? The union seemed like a good way to do it, though now I'm not so sure anymore.

The pressure of making ends meet and the knowledge that others were doing better clearly had an impact on Tomás Quintana, a forklift operator at Camagua who decided to support the union:

> After a while I met people who were doing better than I was. They weren't rich or anything, but [pause] . . . they were more comfortable and had nice things. I started thinking about it and decided that I had to do something about it. But I didn't know what to do, until the guy from the union talked to me. At first I

was nervous about losing my job, but I realized that I could probably find another one, probably making as much as I was making, which was a little over the minimum. We did have medical insurance and I didn't want to lose that — especially with three kids. Anyway, the guy told me that if they fired me, they [the union organizers] would help me get my job back or find me another one. I had my doubts, but I decided to go with them. All I wanted was to have what other people had, nothing more.

From an organizer's perspective the length of time that immigrants have been in the United States is a critical factor. Organizers contend that it is easier to organize undocumented workers who have been living in the United States for at least a year or two. As Rivas explained it,

> Yeah, the longer they've been here, the easier it is to organize them. The ones who've been here for a short time are too scared. No matter what you tell them, no matter how much you reassure them, they — very politely — tell you they're not interested or they'll think about it. I've been organizing for over twenty years and that's always been the case.

Jaime Montalvo, another organizer with many years of experience organizing in Los Angeles, both in the fields and factories, concurs:

> It's not that those who arrived only a little while ago aren't interested. It's just a lot harder to get them, and if you get them, to keep them. They're too skittish. But that's understandable. I've known guys who a year later were the most militant of the bunch, but a year earlier were scared rabbits. . . . I think it's a combination of things. Getting acclimated and realizing that it costs a lot of money to live here. And if they get married and start to raise a family, or once they bring their family, then forget it. Then they listen to you. Not all of them, of course, but the more time they've been here, the more likely they are to want the union.

Several workers confirmed this when they noted that initially they were continuously fearful of being picked up by the INS. Other than trips to and from work, few of them rarely ventured too far from home in their first few months in Los Angeles. The following experience of Jaime Alarcón, one migrant employed as a tape edger at Camagua, is illustrative. He said, laughing,

> I was really scared when I got here. I remember going to get a physical examination for a job and when I walked in, there was a "migra" agent sitting in the waiting area. As it turned out, he was waiting for some guy he had brought in, but I didn't know that then. I picked up a magazine in English and pretended to be reading it. I was probably holding it upside down. When I got out of there I went straight to my uncle's home [where Alarcón was staying] and for a couple of months just went to work and straight home everyday. But after a few more months . . . maybe four or five . . . I didn't think or worry about the "migra" anymore.

Gradually they lost their fear of the "migra" and, subsequently, rarely thought about Immigration or their citizenship status. As a leadman and strong opponent of unionization at Camagua, Alfredo Sánchez, noted, "You're careful, sure, so as not to get picked up by Immigration. But that's at first. In time you lose that initial fear."[18]

In a *Los Angeles Times* article on INS sweeps, Becklund (1985:3) reported that long-term residents were less concerned about the raids: One worker remarked, " 'As long as there is Los Angeles, there will be Latinos coming here to work. Besides, they've never gotten me yet.' " The comment reflects not only the sense of security that accompanies length of residency and the low probability of being apprehended, but also the realization that there is a demand for their labor. In their survey with migrants awaiting deportation, North and Houstoun (1976) found that the longer a migrant had been in the United States, the more likely he was to be a union member.

Permanent settler migrants "have lived and worked in the United States for many years, during which they have adopted U.S. standards of living and have become familiar with U.S. labor laws" (Mines and Kaufman 1985:208). Compared to newcomers, permanent settler migrants are more likely to join unions and defend their rights. It is not citizens of the United States, but rather long-term resident immigrants who are the victims of less-established newcomers. "Employers are able to use the newcomers as components of cost-cutting strategies whose ultimate results are the reduction of wage levels, the degradation of working conditions, and the weakening of unions" (Mines and Kaufman 1985:208). Research on undocumented immigrants in Austin and San Antonio revealed that permanent settlers were less likely to tolerate unfair work practices and "to the extent the settlers represent an increasing proportion of the total indocumentado [undocumented] population, there is a greater likelihood that indocumentado workers will be less tractable to employer control" (Browning and Rodríguez 1985:293–94).

The tendency of longer-term residents to be less tractable can be attributed partly to the extensive kinship and friendship networks immigrants build over time (Mines and Kaufman 1985; Zavella 1987). Compared to those of permanent settlers, the networks of less-established newcomers are less mature and rarely lead to good job contacts and steady employment. The former's networks have become "more important to the success of Mexican workers in the United States than their legal status. An experienced migrant from a well-established network can feel very secure in the United States even if he is undocumented and must occasionally reenter the country after being deported" (Mines and Kaufman 1985:209).

Some of the benefits of unionization also are more appealing to permanent settlers. In this sector of the economy, wage increases won by unions tend to be small. Important union benefits, such as job security, seniority, and pension plans, tend to be long term. Short-term migrants have less to gain and are less inclined to

tolerate periods without work in the event of a strike or termination, however short the period of unemployment. They are not in
it for the long haul. The benefits of unionization are likely to be
more attractive to immigrants prepared to remain in the country — especially with a particular firm — permanently or for an
extended period of time. Furthermore, medical insurance, another
benefit of unionization, is particularly attractive to someone with a
family. At Camagua virtually everyone was married or had children. The workers' medical coverage was clearly an important
issue for them.[19]

For most of Camagua's workers, the United States had become
their new (and for some a second) home, one in which they, not
unlike earlier immigrants, sought to carve out a niche for themselves and secure a better future for their children. In fact, some of
the workers owned their own homes, and several had become
landlords in economically depressed areas of Los Angeles. For
many of their children, Los Angeles, not Mexico or El Salvador,
was the only home they knew.

The desire of workers to remain with one firm as opposed to
selling their labor to the highest bidder emerged repeatedly in the
interview. When I asked him why he did not leave Camagua for a
higher-paying job offered to him by another company, Miguel
Marín responded in a manner virtually identical to others asked
the same question:

MARÍN: I'd rather stay somewhere I know; and anyway, the
company [Camagua] was progressing. I could go somewhere
else, but get laid off or be without work a few months later. That
won't happen at Camagua. Most people prefer to stay in one
place, don't they?

HLD: But what if you had been offered a lot more money
somewhere else?

MARÍN:It had to be *a lot* more! I was offered a dollar or two
more once, but I turned it down. I was lucky that I did, because

two months later the factory closed. But it wasn't all luck. I knew Camagua was doing well and that a lot of factories close down in Los Angeles. I know too many people who have been left on the street. A place I was working in once closed down. I got another job pretty quickly, but then I had to get used to a new routine, new people. I like staying in one place.

The interviews were replete with variations of this and other statements that underscored the importance of job tenure in labor organizing.

Among the more important distinctions between the primary and secondary labor markets particularly relevant to the issue of unionization are the relative security and stability of employment, both of which are greater in the primary sector (Piore 1975). The higher the turnover rate, the more difficult it is to organize a plant. As indicated in Chapter I, one important reason workers are said to be likely to change jobs more often in the secondary sector is that they have few incentives to remain. In this sector, wages tend to be low, employment security tenuous, and jobs dead-end (Edwards 1979:167–168). Citing several studies confirming that secondary employment is associated with shorter job tenures than primary sector employment, Edwards (1979:169) notes (as my own research and the statements by Marín and others suggest) that there is evidence indicating that "some secondary workers stay at their jobs for relatively long periods and are not perpetual job-changers."[20] Furthermore, in paternalistic firms, which Camagua had been prior to the unionization drive, turnover rates are lower and work habits more stable than suggested by labor market segmentation theory (Lawson 1981:47).

Most of the workers at Camagua had been in the United States for at least eight years, and some had lived in Los Angeles for as long as twenty years. At the time of the organizing drive, most of the workers had been with the company for at least five years, some for as long as fifteen years. On average, the length of residency in the United States and job tenures at Camagua were longer for

Mexicans than for Central Americans. The owner and supervisors at Camagua indicated that their turnover rate was relatively low. Management personnel at other companies reported that their turnover was not very high, and was even less so, not surprisingly, in the more skilled jobs.

Joaquín Rivera, an organizer, offered the provocative suggestion that being undocumented may contribute to workers' longer job tenures. Since they have fewer options as undocumented immigrants, especially to move up to better-paying and more desirable jobs, they may remain in a job longer than someone in the same sector with more options. This also suggests that trying to secure better wages and working conditions in their current jobs is a reasonable option to explore first, since other options are likely to include comparable jobs. It should not come as a total surprise, Rivera maintained, that, given the opportunity to organize, and knowing that there are other jobs similar to their own, some undocumented workers opt for unionization. I asked one undocumented worker, Wilfredo Benítez, on strike after the passage of the Immigration Reform and Control Act of 1986 (IRCA), if he did not fear losing his job. He simply responded, "I make the minimum: $3.35 an hour. I can get a job anywhere making that. Why not try to get more here? I could always get another job at $3.35." Pointing down the street, Benítez added, "All I have to do is walk down this street and I'd find something today." Amaro concurred: "A job paying minimum wage you can find on any corner." The same sentiment was expressed by a number of Camagua's workers, including Sonia Domínguez, a sealing machine operator.

> DomíNGUEZ: It's not like I was risking the best job in the world. In fact, instead of joining the union I seriously thought of going somewhere else. But you get used to working somewhere, you make friends, and [pause] . . . well you say you're going to do something and you never get around to it. Maybe I was too lazy. So I struggled with the union.

HLD: And if you lost your job?

DOMÍNGUEZ: I'd get another one.

HLD: Just like that?

DOMÍNGUEZ: Sure, why not? This wasn't my first job here.

HLD: But could you find one as good?

DOMÍNGUEZ: What was so good about it?

HLD: Well . . . you said you had good medical insurance.

DOMÍNGUEZ: That's true, but it wasn't worth the abuse.

The length of time in the country, tenure with a particular firm, and the commitment to remain in both affect the way in which workers see their jobs and themselves. Temporary migrants draw a sharp distinction between work and social identity, with the latter located in their place of origin. "From the perspective of the [temporary] immigrant, the work is essentially asocial: It is purely a means to an end" (Piore 1979:53–54). For native workers, work is both economic and social. Their identity is tied up with their job. Immigrants who settle permanently, unlike temporary migrants, do not work exclusively for money (Piore 1979). Even if they are unable to find less menial work, the manner in which they are treated by employers and supervisors becomes increasingly important. The deterioration of the employer-employee relationship in Camagua and the disatisfaction of workers with the manner in which they were being treated grew as the company grew.

Despite low wages and few avenues for advancement, many workers express loyalty to their firm and identify strongly with the interests of their company (Bailey 1987; Lawson 1981). This had been the case at Camagua and continued to be for a number of workers who felt that union supporters betrayed the owner. As Marco Gitano, one of the leadmen in the foundation department, observed, "The guy had given me a job. How could I support a bunch of people [union organizers] who I didn't know and were interested only in my money [dues]?" Vincente Fernández, an employee in the foam department, called union supporters "in- grates" for turning their backs on Ramírez: "At least we always worked. There were no lay-offs, ever. Even when the factory burned down, he kept everyone. He didn't lay anybody off. And this is how they repaid him?" Armando Peñalosa, a foam cutter, addressed the issue of loyalty even more directly. "This wasn't just a job, and the owner didn't treat us only as his employees. He even ate lunch with us, asked how we were. It was like a family. You don't take care of family problems in the street, do you? You don't bring in strangers. I don't have respect for people like that." These conditions reflect the use of "paternalism as a technique for con- trolling and motivating workers" (Bailey 1987:26).

While this form of labor control was much more prevalent at the turn of the century, these simple systems of control are not histor- ical curiosities, but rather the order of the day in the peripheral sector of the economy. "Found primarily in retail and wholesale trade, light manufacturing, and personal and business services, the small businessman or businesswoman of today operates much like his or her predecessors did a century ago" (Edwards 1979:34). Even in larger companies that had "profited from the general advances in the art of management" (for example, the use of professional consultants or personnel specialists), as Camagua was doing increasingly, "in its fundamentals, simple control persists" (Edwards 1979:35).

The employer-employee relationship described by Bailey (1987) is based on his own and others' research on immigrant workers:

> What emerges from the studies . . . is a picture of a system in which workers, in exchange for certain obligations of the em- ployer, are expected to be loyal, dependable, and willing to work overtime and extra shifts. The central obligation of the pater- nalistic owner appears to be the provision of job security. (Bailey 1987:26)

Eugene Genovese's (1974:144) description of the slave-master relationship, the most extreme form of paternalism, applies, with qualification, of course, to the relationship between Ramírez and his employees prior to 1980:

> For the masters, paternalism meant reciprocal duties within which the master had a duty to provide for his people and to treat them with humanity, and the slaves had a duty to work properly and to do as they were told. Necessarily, the slaves also had, from the white point of view, incurred an obligation to be grateful.

Slaves, however, saw the slaveholder's duty to provide for them as their right. Camagua's workers believed that Ramírez owed them job security, respect, and a wage that would allow them to feed their families. Several workers made statements similar to the following, made by Javier Santiago, who was fired during the campaign:

> SANTIAGO: We weren't asking for anything we didn't have a right to expect. We did what we were told, but he didn't have a right to treat us the way he did.
>
> HLD: How did he treat you?
>
> SANTIAGO: Like animals.
>
> HLD: Was it him or the supervisors that . . .
>
> SANTIAGO: It's the same thing. He's the boss, right? So he's responsible. He should've done something about it. I hear that now he is, but it was too late. He owed us that much. We worked hard for him!

In effect, the owner had violated their implied contract, or agreement.

The master-slave relationship was an "uneven agreement" in

which slaves would accept punishment for a wrongdoing and become enraged if punished unfairly. They also resented insults and
would withdraw, displaying a feeling of betrayal. "The slaves'
acceptance of paternalism, therefore, signaled acceptance of an
imposed white domination within which they drew their own
lines, asserted rights, and preserved their self-respect" (Genovese
1974:146–47). While the analogy between slavery and Camagua
paints a more benign picture of the former and a more malig-
nant one of Camagua than are warranted, the juxtaposition is
a useful one in understanding paternalism in power relationships. A significant point of departure is that Camagua's workers
had options Africans in slavery did not have, and unionization
was one.[21]

Ramírez, like many other owners who employed paternalism as
a form of labor control, addressed workers by their first names, discussed their personal problems with them, and generally treated
them with respect. "Essentially paternal employers attempt to join
family and work symbolically with themselves as the authority"
(Lawson 1981:48). Ramírez preferred to think of the company as a
family. The following assessment of entrepreneurial control in
small firms early in the twentieth century applies in the Camagua
case: "Workers undoubtedly were oppressed and exploited by such
employers, but they also became enmeshed in a whole network of
personal relations. They had someone with whom to identify"
(Edwards 1979:26). Even as the company expanded, Ramírez attempted to maintain these personal relationships. But this became
increasingly difficult as the company and work force expanded, and
as he became more successful.

The earlier, closer personal relations between Ramírez and his
workers concealed fundamental class differences between them,
which the union sought to exploit: "The personal ties that owners
of small businesses established with their workers in many cases
tended to obscure the real class differences between them. Loyalty had a direct and personal meaning for workers, and many
were reluctant to break the bonds it formed" (Edwards 1979:27).

These ties tended to divide workers and make unionization more difficult. "Wherever paternalism exists, it undermines solidarity among the oppressed by linking them as individuals to their oppressors" (Genovese 1974:5). Neither the McCormick Harvesting Machine Company nor Pabst Brewing Company became unionized at the turn of the century until personal ties between the employer and employees were weakened and class differences exposed (Edwards 1979:27).

In the case of Camagua, the union attempted, with some success, to reveal and highlight these very class differences that had been hidden by the employer's personal relationship with many of the workers and their common Latino ethnicity. Organizers distributed among workers photocopies of an article on the owner in a Spanish-language newspaper to demonstrate how they were not profiting from the owner's financial success (and their own labor) and constantly reminded them that he was becoming rich at their expense, or "on their backs." Elena Salas, a long-time employee of the company, claimed that she resented the fact that while the owner was struggling to establish the business, the workers "stuck with him. But when he made it, he forgot us. Why didn't he share his good fortune with us? We helped him get it, didn't we?"

At Camagua, a number of developments connected to the growth of the company weakened the paternalistic relationship and made the company more susceptible to unionization. The company was growing rapidly. It was producing an increasingly popular softside waterbed and had made inroads into markets waterbed manufacturers had not been able to penetrate previously. As the company expanded, the work force grew, as did the number of workers with less time at the company.[22] Workers became more removed from the owner, who had been more visible and actively involved in the day-to-day operation of the plant in the first ten years of the company's existence. The effect was reminiscent of the transition earlier in the twentieth century by many large companies from a simple to a more complex system of labor control.

Great organizational distance and increasing differences in life situations between capitalist (or managers) and workers generally weakened the extent of personal contact and identification. . . . Thus the expansion of formerly entrepreneurial firms undermined the personal sway that an individual capitalist could hold over his workers. The method of control came into conflict with the requirements of production. (Edwards 1979:29–30)

Camagua's success meant more workers and more levels of supervision; the owner relied increasingly on supervisors to serve, in effect, as his surrogates. "Hierarchical control was based on the concept that each boss — whether a foreman, supervisor, or manager — would re-create in his shop the situation of the capitalist under entrepreneurial control" (Edwards 1979:31). The rough transition from a simple system of control to a more complex hierarchical one contributed significantly to the disintegration of the paternalistic relationship between Ramírez and many of his workers and to the emergence of dignity as a key factor in the organizing campaign.

In attempting to identify the primary reasons workers opted for the unionization of Camagua, both promanagement and prounion forces repeatedly cited the abusive treatment of workers by supervisors as the principal catalyst. Interviews with workers and organizers from other plants and other unions indicated that disrespectful and inhumane treatment by management was typically a critical factor in decisions by workers to organize. Fernando González's assessment of his fellow supervisor, Basilio Tirado, is illustrative of one version, shared by many of Camagua's workers and supervisors, of what happened at Camagua:

He especially treated people with little respect, and he was vindictive. It was difficult to talk to him. He yelled at people in front of others, instead of taking them aside. When the union started to come in, instead of letting up, [Tirado] pressured people even more. When he did, thirty supporters turned into ninety, into one hundred and fifty.

The tendency to focus on bread-and-butter issues in labor-management conflicts can sometimes obscure the importance of the human relations dimension. Ramírez certainly became aware of it, even if after the fact.

Asked why the union targeted his factory, Ramírez responded that they "hit" him when the business was growing. He contends that he was most vulnerable at this time:

> When you're an entrepreneur like myself, and you're growing, you pay less and less attention to the work force. You don't realize that the people you have managing that work force are not experienced or educated enough to do it. Then they mistreat the worker. I don't deny that some of my leadmen mistreated workers. . . . You can't call people dummies, kick them in the butt.

While the inexperience in some cases and the poor training of the supervisors was a critical factor, the significance of this factor was intimately tied to the issue of respect. The owner recognized that, despite their legal status, his workers expected to be treated with respect, and he understood how this was tied to the issue of job security:

> Security is an important thing here. If a worker is mistreated, he doesn't feel secure. If a leadman has an argument with his wife and takes it out on the workers, they in turn feel that if it keeps up, soon they won't be able to keep their job. The union then tells them that with a union they can't lose their job. So they go with the union.[23]

Manuela Guindín expressed her anger with the disrespectful manner in which the owner's son, whom she had seen "grow up from a child into a man," treated her on one occasion:

> He tried to humiliate me, but I called him on it. I told him that just because he has had everything since the day he was born, it didn't give him a right to put us down. I told him that that wasn't

the way it was. Don't forget, I'm a human being. You could have a lot of money and I may never be able to have anything. When you no longer need my labor and services, you can keep your dirty money, because you don't pay me shit! I give you my lungs for the miserly wages that you pay me!

The interview was conducted two years after the incident, yet the anger and hurt were still evident.

Fortunately for the union, paternalism as a form of labor control is relatively fragile.

Factors that serve to reduce worker dependency on the firm, or provide alternative "world views," or which force management to act inconsistently with employer expectations, may all serve to undermine it: workers' consciousness and organizational solidarity may form very quickly. (Lawson 1981:49)

The rapid growth of the company, which forced the owner to behave contrary to workers' expectations; the appearance of the union on the scene; and the union's effectiveness in severing what personal ties remained between the owner and many of the workers served to undermine this fragile form of labor control and expedite the organizational solidarity of the workers.

While many immigrants may live in the shadows and suffer a multitude of indignities because of their immigration status, many have stepped out and have demanded to be treated in a just and humane manner. The workers at Camagua did just this when they voted for union representation and engaged in a protracted and successful struggle to obtain a contract.

Jesús Alvarez, a leadman opposed to the union, observed,

They [the workers] weren't afraid of anything. You have to admire them. They weren't afraid of the owner or the supervisors. They stood up to the supervisors. They [supervisors] could no longer get away with what they had been doing. . . . They really supported one another. The ones fired at the same time were particularly united. There were two round tables with about fourteen people.

The union's commitment to organize Camagua and the sense of security Camagua's workers derived from the legal rights they learned that they had were key factors in many workers' participation in the campaign — and its ultimate success.

Chapter IV

Undocumented Workers and the Law

A critical factor in the unionization of Camagua was the role of the union, both in the resources it invested and the tactics it employed. Camagua was not unique in this respect. The few improvements Mexican immigrant workers were able to achieve in their conditions of work prior to World War II were owed in considerable measure to the formation of their own unions and the commitment of leftist unions. During most of this period, the AFL sat on the sidelines. The Industrial Workers of the World (IWW), or Wobblies, "failed, and miserably so, in . . . fashioning the collective discontent of farmworkers into a viable instrument of economic change, much less revolution" (Daniel 1981:85). But they were among the first to attempt to organize farm workers. The Trade Union Unity League (TUUL), established by the Communist Party in opposition to the AFL, helped to revive and expand the unionization of farm workers during the 1930s (Jamieson 1976). The Cannery and Agricultural Workers Industrial Union (CAWIU) was also active in California's fields (Daniel 1981).

In the second half of the 1930s, the Congress of Industrial Organizations (CIO)–affiliated United Cannery, Agricultural, Packing, and Allied Workers of America (UCAPAWA) was formed to lead an organizing drive of agricultural and allied industries workers (Daniel 1981). The UCAPAWA was joined by the Confederación de Uniones de Campesinos y Obreros Mexicanos del Estado de California (CUCOM), the Confederation of Mexican Farmworkers and Laborers Unions of the State of California (Acuña 1988), which had won some concessions from growers between 1935 and 1937 and had set the stage for the UCAPAWA's statewide campaign by working effectively with other ethnic groups (Jamieson 1976).

The UCAPAWA concentrated on cannery and pack-shed workers. These workers, unlike laborers in the fields, were not migratory, could afford higher union dues, and were protected by the NLRA. But the UCAPAWA had to compete with the AFL for these workers. "The A.F. of L.'s most important allies in its jurisdictional contest with pro-CIO insurgents during the spring of 1937 were employers in the canning and packing industries, many of whom had resigned themselves to the unionization of their employees and believed that the federation was the lesser of two evils" (Daniel 1981:279). The only support farm workers received from the UCAPAWA was occasional modest assistance during strikes. "In the end, the CIO adopted the view, long held by the A.F. of L., that agricultural workers did not constitute a labor problem as much as a social problem" (Daniel 1981:281). It was a problem that government, not organized labor, had to address.

This view is shared in the 1990s by many unionists, as evidenced by the AFL-CIO's support of some key provisions of the IRCA. It is a position that organizer George Higgins said, "gave aid and comfort to the enemy" — the employer. Despite divisions with the ranks of organized labor on the issue, the CWU and many unionists organizing in Los Angeles treat the presence of unorganized immigrant workers as a labor problem, remedied only through the unionization of this segment of the workforce. The problem has a social dimension as well. But some unionists argued, Rivas among them, that this too organized labor can and should address by helping immigrant workers secure higher wages, improved job security, better treatment by supervisors, and decent benefits.

Rivas envisioned a daycare center in the middle of the garment district, subsidized by unions and employers, to provide low-cost childcare for garment workers. Whether he believed this was a real possibility was not clear to me, but his point was that unions had to address the work- and non-work-related needs of immigrants and other workers if they were to recapture lost ground. In effect, there was no such thing as a non-work-related need. Organized labor's commitment, Rivas underscored, had to be material as well as rhetorical.

Rivas received considerable support for the Camagua campaign from the international offices in New York, but it was never enough, and creative bookkeeping by the local was sometimes required to make ends meet. The resistance the CWU encountered from Ramírez required a serious and sustained commitment by the union — and in this instance the union came through. Adamantly opposed to unions, because he felt they lowered production and did not know how to run a successful business, Ramírez fought aggressively to keep his company union free.[1] He may have invested more than one million dollars to fight the union, but the union, in turn, may have spent in excess of five hundred thousand dollars, according to Rivas. In this respect, Ramírez responded as many other employers respond to unionization campaigns. Ramírez was unsuccessful in his attempt to fend off the union. But in the past twenty years, to the chagrin of organized labor, employers have been extremely successful in their efforts at resistance. "Despite considerable differences among studies, . . . virtually all tell the same story: managerial opposition to unionism, and illegal campaign tactics in particular, are a major, if not the major, determinant of NLRB election results" (Freeman and Medoff 1984:233).

As indicated earlier, to fight the union, Ramírez engaged the services of Rafael Hernández, a labor consultant. Hernández unsuccessfully employed a number of tactics to dissuade workers from supporting the union and organized a procompany demonstration outside the plant. (A blown-up photograph of this demonstration hangs in one of the factory's work areas.) The company fired eight workers involved in an altercation at the plant gate, later agreeing to a cash settlement in lieu of reinstatement. Ramírez also fired another thirty workers for slow downs, refused to sign a contract until nearly the end of the negotiating period, and prolonged the entire process by appealing the elections at the state and federal levels.

The union and workers were equally determined to obtain a contract. Rivas, in fact, did not recall an organizing drive in which the union had invested as much labor, time, and money. The union used workplace tactics, such as slow downs, the chanting of campaign slogans during short work stoppages, and constant picketing outside the factory gates to pressure the company, but it was the corporate campaign that bore the most fruit for the union and workers.

The union succeeded in making the issue more than simply a labor dispute, drawing in community activists, including clergy, concerned with the rights of immigrants and Latinos. One of the campaign's major events, described earlier, was a mass, or religious ceremony, which was held outside the main plant gate half an hour before the end of the day shift and was attended by the vast majority of workers and a number of community activists. Other unions lent moral and material support as well. The union also tried, unsuccessfully, to get local Latino politicians and the mayor to pressure the owner to give in to the workers' demands. The most effective tool of the corporate campaign, however, was the boycott of Camagua's waterbeds.

Workers stood outside retail stores that sold the Camagua product, passing out leaflets; union representatives called other retailers and the media. Some of the organizers and workers were convinced that in the more affluent areas and malls, such as Beverly Hills, the sight of a group of Mexican immigrants would be enough to prompt many retailers to discontinue the sale of Camagua waterbeds. In many instances they were correct. As Kersey put it, "You win a boycott by making the selling of something a dirty thing or very inconvenient. Here it was if you sell this waterbed, you'll have a group of 'dirty Latinos' walking in front of your door. Their racism worked to our advantage." A couple of the retailers even made ethnic slurs about Ramírez to Kersey.

At one point, the union had eight organizers and the coordinator of the corporate campaign and boycott working on the campaign. All of the organizers spoke Spanish, but more important, they were all Latinos and several had immigrated from Mexico or other Latin American countries. The fact that the organizers not only knew the language, but were themselves, for the most part, Mexican or Central American, facilitated the unionization process.

I observed Rivas on several occasions talking to largely Mexican groups of immigrant workers who were contemplating unionization, and I saw the knack, described to me by several people, that he had for organizing these workers. He spoke their language. Not simply Spanish. It was the rhythm of his speech, his stories, his body language that they understood, not just the words. He explained the process of organizing in a deliberate manner, injecting jokes or reminiscences from home at just the right moments to make a point, to clarify something, to get them to trust him, to relax them. His stories and jokes evoked laughter and approving nods as the workers looked at and seemed to connect with one another.

Research on southern and eastern European immigrants in the early part of the twentieth century reveals that the more effective organizers were members of the same ethnic group as the workers they were trying to organize, in part because the ideas and procedures being explained often were "fairly abstract and intricate" (Asher 1982:332). A person of the same cultural background could explain these ideas more effectively than someone who was simply an interpreter. Every union I contacted in Los Angeles that organizes immigrant workers has several, and in a number of cases a preponderance of, Latino organizers — and Rivas, while recognized by a number of his counterparts in other unions as one of the best organizers of immigrant workers in the city, was not the only one with this knack. Both the Latino composition of the work force and the low status of organizers in the union hierarchy have contributed to a substantial increase in the number of Latino organizers.[2]

Workers responded positively to Anglo organizers as well. As José García explained, "We expect fellow Latinos to stand up and fight for us, but when a *gabacho* does it, it makes us feel good and makes us want to fight a little harder. If he's willing to fight for us, we just can't sit back." Kersey, who spoke Spanish, was particularly popular among the workers and was remembered fondly in the interviews. He, and other Anglo organizers, recognized the importance of conversing in the workers' language and as Jerry Gordon, an organizer for another union, put it, their "culture."

The response of Camagua's workers to female organizers was an interesting and generally positive one. Luis Otero, a Salvadoran worker fired by Ramírez, said, "If a woman is prepared to struggle and to fight, to yell and scream, then how can I, a man, not do at least as much?" As Otero's remark suggests, the militancy of the female workers and organizers was a source of pressure for some of the male workers. Several of the pro-union workers, while accepting the participation of their female coworkers and the leadership of Celia Colón and Cecilia Durán, never felt completely comfortable with either. Ignacio Mejías, a worker in his late forties, expressed his discomfort by commenting on the "vulgar" way in which Durán sometimes expressed herself. "She talks like a man. She says vulgar things like *pendejo* or that son of a bitch, and I don't think a woman should talk like that. I'm old-fashioned." Four other male workers expressed similar sentiments about the "proper" role of women, both generally and specifically in the campaign, but in neither Mejías's case nor in the case of the other workers' did these sentiments have a deleterious effect on their participation in the campaign. Each, in fact, recognized the important contributions of the female organizers to the campaign. Colón and Durán formed strong and lasting bonds with a number of workers, female and male.

Union representatives justified the unusual resources poured into the Camagua campaign by arguing that they wanted to send a message to employers in the bedding and other industries that immigrant workers were indeed organizable. How much impact the message had is difficult to ascertain. But the small amount of organizing done by either the CWU or other unions within the industry since suggests that the impact was not very great.

The union's single-minded commitment to organize Camagua was indispensable to the success of the campaign. But whether the CWU and most unions have the capacity to engage in many of these long and costly organizing campaigns is a critical question. Kersey recalls a comment by the organizing director in the CWU's international offices in New York City to the effect that Camagua for them was a "black hole. Any more [Camaguas] and the union would fold."[3] In this respect, Camagua may be the exception that proves the rule, that is, if the organization of marginal plants and workers, including immigrant workers from Mexico and Central America, requires inordinate amounts of resources, the cost may make their organization prohibitive. The growth in light manufacturing and the service industries, and projected increases in the Latino and immigrant workforce, however, seem to offer few choices to organized labor. The Latino population in Los Angeles is expected to rise from 25 percent to 40 percent of the city's population by the end of the twentieth century. By the year 2010, people of color are expected to constitute 60 percent of the city's population (Lockwood and Leinberger 1988).

The union's involvement at Camagua took many forms. The legal information and resources with which the union provided the workers were particularly important in helping to dissipate the fear of termination among Camagua's workers. While the fear of losing a job is well-founded statistically and serves as an obstacle to unionization, often it is compounded by undocumented workers' belief that they have no rights in the event of a wrongful termination. Organizers noted that, among the first things they communicate to workers is that the workers are protected by labor laws, despite their undocumented status. Briggs (1978:218) is correct in asserting that, "in the long run, the presence of a growing number of workers who are denied political rights as well as minimum legal and job protection is a sure prescription for eventual trouble."

Undocumented workers, however, are protected by the NLRA and the Fair Labor Standards Act (FLSA), despite their citizenship status.[4]

Part of the explanation for workers' lack of concern about their legal status no doubt lies in organizers' ability to anticipate and respond to concerns about citizenship status and rights as workers. By providing them with information about their rights, organizers have been able to avert potential problems. As several organizers indicated, they have to do additional work because of the workers' undocumented status (for example, inform them of their rights and assure them of legal assistance), but otherwise it is no different to organize them than to organize workers with documents. The following assessment by Rick García, an organizer from another union, is illustrative:

> Some people say undocumented workers are difficult to organize. I think they're wrong. . . . It's that you have to do a little more educating of that worker than you do for documented workers. For example, an undocumented worker assumes that he or she has no legal rights — any legal rights under labor law or any law of the country. So you have to sit them down and educate them. You have to tell them. You have to show them. You have to prove to them that they do. So it takes a little more time. That's really the biggest difference.

García and several other organizers, in fact, contended that undocumented workers were often more receptive to unionization and more militant than their documented counterparts or native workers. Salvadoran immigrants, they argued, were more militant than Mexican workers, but the former were not indispensable to the success of a campaign. CWU's organizers saw little difference in the Camagua campaign between Mexican and Salvadoran immigrants in this respect.

In the Camagua campaign, workers clearly were emboldened (and surprised) by the knowledge that they were protected by the country's labor laws. A fundamental concern of organizers and immigrants-rights advocates has always been the protection of undocumented workers under the NLRA and FLSA. Prior to the IRCA, unions relied on some key court decisions to assure undocumented workers of their right to organize and their protection under the NLRA. The assurance that they were protected by the country's labor laws, despite their undocumented status, served to calm fears and encourage workers to demand their rights. Jorge Irrizary, a strong opponent of the union, observed, "Once you are in the country, you have the same rights as anyone else. Immigration is not a problem here."

In 1979, the United States Court of Appeals for the Ninth Circuit, ruled in *NLRB v. Apollo Tire Co., Inc.* (1979) that "undocumented aliens" were "employees" as defined by the NLRA and entitled to reinstatement. In March 1977, Hilda Niz, the mother of an Apollo Tire Company employee, complained to the company's general manager that her son had not received overtime pay to which he was entitled. Failing to receive satisfaction from the company, Niz complained to the Wage and Hour Division of the Department of Labor on April 18. She was given some forms in Spanish, which she distributed to workers. Seven of the employees completed and submitted the forms to the compliance officer.

On April 22, the company fired six of the seven complainants, claiming as the reason a decrease in sales and buildup in inventory. The seventh was not fired because he was employed under an alias and the company, consequently, did not know that he was one of the complainants. Eight days later the company told the discharged employees to return to work; only two reported. When two others attempted to return three days later, the company refused to rehire them.

The NLRB found the company in violation of Sections 8(a)(1) and (a)(4) of the NLRA and ordered Apollo to cease and desist from, among other things, "in any . . . manner interfering with, restraining or coercing employees in the exercise of their rights under Section 7 of the NLRA" (*NLRB v. Apollo Tire* 1979:1182). Section 7 of the Act reads, "Employees shall have the right to self-organize, to form, join or assist labor organizations, to bargain collectively through representatives of their own choosing and to engage in concerted activities, for the purpose of collective bargaining or other mutual aid or protection." Section 8 of the NLRA "gave meaning" to section 7 by stipulating that certain employer practices were illegal, or "unfair labor practices" (Yates 1987:23). Sections 8(a)(1) and (a)(4) refer, respectively, to interfering with, restraining or coercing workers in their rights under section 7 and discharging or otherwise discriminating against an employee because he or she has filed charges or given testimony (U.S. Congress, National Labor Relations Act: Sections 158[a][1] and [4]).

The company argued that covering illegal aliens under the NLRA conflicted with the spirit and provisions of the Immigration and Nationality Act of 1952 (INA). Apollo's lawyers argued that when Congress enacted the NLRA it intended to exclude aliens without the proper authorization to work in the United States. The court pointed out, however, that the NLRB had consistently ruled that undocumented workers were covered and Congress had never questioned the NLRB's interpretation and application of the statute. The definition of "employee" in section 2(3) of the NLRA is a broad one, and undocumented immigrants are not among the exceptions.[5]

In his decision, Circuit Judge Eugene A. Wright, writing for the majority, cited *NLRB v. Sure-Tan* (1978), in which the seventh circuit court ruled that certifying a union voted in by "illegal aliens" did not, as the company claimed, conflict with the INA. The circuit court noted that no federal immigration statutes prohibited employers from hiring undocumented immigrants or prohibited these immigrants from working and exercising rights guaranteed by the NLRA. While it was illegal to harbor undocumented immigrants, employment, according to the INA, did not constitute harboring. Judge Wright also noted that in *Matthews v. Díaz* (1975), cited in *NLRB v. Sure-Tan* (1978), the Supreme Court had implied that Congress could, if it wished, "extend privileges to illegal aliens." The majority also disagreed with the company on the impact of treating undocumented immigrants as employees, as defined by the NLRA.

> Were we to hold the NLRA inapplicable to illegal aliens, employers would be encouraged to hire such persons in hopes of circumventing the labor laws. The result would be more work for illegal aliens and violations of the immigration laws would be encouraged. (*NLRB v. Apollo Tire Co., Inc.* 1979:1183)

In the *Apollo* case, the company cited in its defense, section 2805 of the California Labor Code (the Arnett Bill), which made it illegal to knowingly hire undocumented workers. This section of the California code, however, was declared unconstitutional and the state's labor commissioner was enjoined from enforcing it in *Dolores Canning Company, Inc. v. Howard* (1974) (Calavita 1982).[6] Wright concluded that the NLRB was correct in its ruling, but if section 2805 of the California Labor Code was found to be enforceable in the future, Apollo could petition for a modification of the order.

The Arnett Bill was the first piece of legislation enacted by a state legislature sanctioning employers for knowingly hiring undocumented immigrants. The law had been remanded to the California courts by the Supreme Court, in order to determine whether applying this section of the labor code would conflict with any federal laws. No action was taken. The law was receiving increasingly stiff opposition from various quarters and thus became a political liability for virtually anyone supporting it. The law "disappeared into legal oblivion" (Calavita 1982:50).

In 1984, the United States Supreme Court handed down a decision that bore directly on the unionization of undocumented workers. In *Sure-Tan, Inc. v. NLRB* (1984), the Supreme Court, affirming the seventh circuit court's decision in *NLRB v. Sure-Tan* (1978), held that undocumented workers were protected by the NLRA. On December 10, 1976, seven workers in Sure-Tan, a Chicago firm, elected as their collective-bargaining representative, the Chicago Leather Workers Union, Local 431, Amalgamated Meatcutters and Butcher Workmen of North America. Shortly after the election, the employer, John Surak, cursed the employees who voted for the union and asked them if they had valid immigration documents. Six of the seven did not. Surak objected to the elections on the basis of these workers' undocumented status. He also admitted knowledge of the workers' illegal presence months before the election and signed an affidavit to that effect. The NLRB overruled Surak's objection and certified the union. Surak then called the INS. This resulted in the voluntary departure of five workers.

In February and March of 1977, the NLRB issued complaints alleging that Surak had committed a number of unfair labor practices. On March 29, Sure-Tan sent the five employees letters in Mexico offering them reinstatement, provided that doing so would not expose the company to any violations of immigration laws. The offer was to remain open through May 1, 1977.

The unfair labor practice charges were heard by an Administrative Law Judge (ALJ) and he concluded that Sure-Tan had violated sections 8(a)(1) and (3) of the NLRA. Section (8)(3) provides that an employer commits an unfair labor practice if he or she discriminates against a worker "to encourage or discourage membership in a labor organization." The ALJ found that Surak investigated his employees status because they supported the union. Surak knew that the workers in question did not have the proper documents.

The ALJ recommended that the workers be offered reinstatement, that the offer be held open for a six-month period, and that the company give them backpay for at least a four-week period, as compensation for their unlawful discharge. The ALJ did not believe that they were entitled to the usual backpay remedy because normally backpay was tolled during periods when workers were unavailable for work. On appeal, the seventh circuit court agreed that Sure-Tan had committed unfair labor practices in violation of the NLRA and that the discharged workers were entitled to six months' backpay and reinstatement. The offer was to be made in Spanish and left open for a four-year period, in order to give the former employees time to enter the country legally. The company petitioned the Supreme Court for review.

The Supreme Court, as noted, upheld the lower court's decision. The Court observed that, in the past, the NLRB had consistently held that undocumented immigrants were "employees" within the meaning of section 2(3) of the NLRA and since the board, as the agency Congress created to administer the act, had been assigned the task of defining "employee," it was "entitled to considerable deference" (*Sure-Tan, Inc. v. NLRB* 1984:742). Furthermore, the majority reasoned that covering these workers was consistent with the act's stated purpose to encourage and protect the collective-bargaining process.

> If undocumented alien employees were excluded from participation in union activities and from protections against employer intimidation, there would be created a subclass of workers without a comparable stake in the collective goals of their legally resident co-workers, thereby eroding the unity of all the employees and impeding effective collective bargaining. Thus, the Board's categorization of undocumented aliens as protected employees furthers the purposes of the NLRA. (*Sure-Tan, Inc. v. NLRB* 1984:743)[7]

The Court argued that if undocumented workers were left unprotected against unfair labor practices by employers, this would be an incentive for employers to hire them. If the demand for these workers declined as a consequence, then this would serve to discourage undocumented immigration, the justices concluded.

Justice Sandra Day O'Connor, writing for the majority, observed that Congress had not passed legislation making it illegal to hire undocumented immigrants or making it a criminal offense for an undocumented immigrant to work in the United States. "Since the employment relationship between an employer and an undocumented alien is hence not illegal under the INA," O'Connor wrote, "there is no reason to conclude that application of the NLRA to employment practices affecting such aliens would necessarily conflict with the terms of the INA" (*Sure-Tan, Inc. v. NLRB* 1984:743–44). The court then turned to the question of whether an unfair labor practice had taken place in this case.

The Court noted that Sure-Tan did not dispute its illegal attempts to discourage workers from unionizing. What the company did argue was that it was not their reporting of the workers to the INS that caused their departure from the United States, but rather their status as undocumented workers that was the "proximate cause" of their departure. The Supreme Court rejected the argument, noting that had it not been for the company's actions, the workers would have continued working indefinitely and that Surak foresaw this outcome, since he knew about the workers' status and called the INS only after the union's victory was assured. This was not to say that a company could not report an employee to the INS. That, in fact, O'Connor wrote, should be encouraged.

> It is only when the evidence establishes that the reporting of the presence of an illegal alien employee is in retaliation for the employee's protected union activity that the Board finds a violation of Section 8(a)(3). Absent this specific finding of anti-union animus, it would not be an unfair labor practice to report or discharge an undocumented alien employee. . . . Such a holding is consistent with the policies of both the INA and the NLRA. (*Sure-Tan, Inc. v. NLRB* 1984:745)

The Court, however, did not agree with the lower court's decision concerning remedies.

The Supreme Court found that backpay remedies should be tailored to the actual (and not speculative), compensable injuries suffered by the workers who were fired. The six-month period selected by the seventh circuit court was, by its own admission, "obviously conjectural." The majority of the justices approved the reinstatement of the workers upon their legal readmittance to the United States. Only in this way, the justices explained, could a potential conflict with the INA be avoided. With reference to computing backpay, the Court held that employees had to be "deemed 'unavailable' for work (and the accrual of backpay there-fore tolled) during any period when they were not lawfully entitled to be present and employed in the United States" (*Sure-Tan, Inc. v. NLRB* 1984:750). The justices acknowledged that the "practical workings of the immigration laws" perhaps made it impossible for the NLRB to resort to its most effective remedies in cases such as these, but this was something Congress and not the Court had to address. "By directing the Board to impose a minimum backpay award without regard to the employees' actual economic losses or legal availability for work, the Court of Appeals plainly ex-ceeded its limited authority under the Act" (*Sure-Tan, Inc. v. NLRB* 1984:751).

Justices William J. Brennan, Thurgood Marshall, Harry A. Blackmun, and John Paul Stevens III felt that the remedy was too limited, preferring to uphold the lower court's award of six months' backpay even though the workers were unavailable to work during the period. Brennan, writing for the minority, argued that the majority failed to address the "disturbing anomaly" it created by holding that undocumented aliens were protected as "employees" within the meaning of the act, but depriving them, in effect, of any remedy when their rights were violated.

The ninth circuit court subsequently relied on the Supreme Court's *Sure-Tan* decision to uphold a labor arbitrator's decision to order reinstatement and backpay to two workers a company had fired for failure to provide proof of legal status in the United States. In this case, the Bevles Company, Inc., argued that the arbitrator had exceeded his authority by granting reinstatement and backpay to two workers the company had fired for not being in the country legally (*Bevles Company, Inc. v. Teamsters Local 986* 1986).

The company's vice-president had received an unsolicited news-letter, in which the attorney who authored it suggested that in California it was unlawful to employ undocumented immigrants. The company sent a memo to all of its workers requiring that they show proof of legal status in the United States. Two machine shop employees who failed to produce the appropriate documents were fired. Teamsters Local 986 filed a grievance on behalf of the workers, claiming that the workers had been fired without just cause.

The company based its decision on section 2805 of the California Labor Code, cited in the unsolicited newsletter.

2805.a. No employer shall knowingly employ an alien who is not entitled to lawful residence in the United States if such employment would have an adverse effect on lawful resident workers.

b. A person found guilty of a violation of subdivision (a) is punishable by a fine of not less than two hundred dollars ($200) nor more than five hundred dollars ($500) for each offense.

c. The foregoing provisions shall not be a bar to civil action against the employer based upon violation (a). (Calavita 1982:3)

The attorney for one of the workers had advised the company, in writing, that this section of the state code had been declared unconstitutional and was not being enforced. The arbitrator ruled in favor of the union, noting that the employer would not have been criminally liable for failing to fire the two workers. Both were entitled to reinstatement, but one of the workers was denied back-pay for using his cousin's name and social security number. The arbitrator's award was confirmed in a federal district court, but the company appealed to the United States Court of Appeal for the Ninth Circuit.

The circuit court affirmed the lower court's decision confirming the arbitrator's award.

We hold that the arbitrator's award of reinstatement and back-pay notwithstanding the immigration status of the employees neither violates a clearly defined public policy nor is in manifest disregard of the law. Neither the company nor its employees are subject to any criminal or civil liability under federal law arising from their employment relationship. (*Bevles Company, Inc., v. Teamsters Local 986.* 1986:1392–93)

The circuit court cited the *Sure-Tan* decision to support its conclusion that undocumented workers were protected by the NLRA, it was not illegal to hire undocumented immigrants, and it was not unlawful for these workers to accept employment in the United States.

Bevles also referred to the *Sure-Tan* decision, in an attempt to support its claim that the remedy granted by the arbitrator was prohibited. The ninth circuit court rejected this claim as well, noting that in the *Sure-Tan* case the workers who had been fired had left the country and, thus, offering them reinstatement and backpay would have encouraged them to return illegally. This was not the case here, since the discharged workers were already in the United States.

The decision by the ninth circuit court was two to one in favor of affirming the district court's confirmation of the arbitrator's award, with Judge Sneed dissenting. He interpreted the *Sure-Tan* decision differently. In his opinion, the justices in the *Sure-Tan* decision stipulated clearly that NLRA remedies had to be reconciled with immigration laws. Sneed quoted Justice O'Connor to argue that reinstatement and entitlement to backpay turned on whether the workers were "lawfully entitled to be present and employed in the United States" (*Bevles Company, Inc. v. Teamsters Local 986.* 1986:1394). Their presence in the United States did not satisfy the Supreme Court's requirement of legal reentry. Otherwise, Sneed maintained, the justices "would have adopted a position that permitted reinstatement and back pay at such time as the employees once more were available to work without regard to their status as illegal aliens" (*Bevles Company, Inc., v. Teamsters Local 986.* 1986:1394).

The ninth circuit court revisited the issue of undocumented status and employee protections under the NLRA in *Local 512, Warehouse and Office Workers' Union, ILGWU, AFL-CIO, et al. v.*

NLRB (1986). In this case, the circuit court once again upheld an NLRB finding that an employer had violated the NLRA. The circuit court found, however, that the NLRB was incorrect in amending the ALJ's order of reinstatement and backpay by requiring workers to show proof of legal status. The employer in this case, Felbro, Inc., manufactured wire and tubular displays in South Gate, California. In August 1981, workers elected Local 512 as their bargaining agent. In the period between the union election and the NLRB's certification of the results, Felbro laid off three employees without prior notification to the union. In addition, negotiators for the company and the union had agreed on the terms of a collective-bargaining agreement, subject to ratification by the members of the union. The company refused to execute the agreement after it was ratified by the membership, claiming that it, the company, had repudiated the contract before it had been notified by the union of its ratification.

The ALJ found that Felbro had violated the act by refusing to abide by and give effect to the collective bargaining agreement and ordered that the fired employees be reinstated and given backpay, the contract be implemented retroactively, and workers be reimbursed for any loss in wages and benefits resulting from the company's failure to implement the contract in a timely fashion. While adopting the ALJ's conclusions concerning the violation of the act, the NLRB amended the ALJ's remedial order by requiring workers to show proof of legal status. The board cited *Sure-Tan* and interpreted the Supreme Court's ruling on reinstatement and backpay in a manner consistent with Judge Breezer's interpretation of *Bevles*. Local 512 petitioned the ninth circuit court for review on the NLRB's remedy order.

Judge Pregerson, writing the majority opinion for the circuit court, upheld the NLRB's finding that Felbro had violated sections 8(a)(5) and (a)(1) of the NLRA by not notifying the union that it had laid off three members and by refusing "to execute the agreed contract." On the remedy order, however, the ninth circuit court concluded that requiring proof of legal status was unlawful.

The NLRB's decision to condition Felbro's payment of backpay upon proof of each discriminated worker's legal status in the United States [was] inconsistent with both the NLRA and the immigration laws. For this reason, we deny enforcement of the remedy portion of the order and remand the order to the Board for appropriate modification. (*Local 512, Warehouse and Office Workers' Union, ILGWU, AFL-CIO, et al. v. NLRB* 1986:709)

Pregerson wrote that the Supreme Court's decision in *Sure-Tan* did not address the issue of backpay for undocumented workers who were available for work and had not been subject to INS proceedings. The board's award in *Sure-Tan*, Pregerson said, was speculative because no one knew how long the workers would be unavailable to work. In the *Felbro* case, the lost wages owed to the discriminatees was actual and not speculative since they were in the country and working at Felbro. Pregerson observed, "The Supreme Court in Sure-Tan gave no indication that it was overruling a significant line of precedent that disregards a discriminatee's legal status, as opposed to availability to work, in determining his or her eligibility for backpay" (*Local 512, Warehouse and Office Workers' Union, ILGWU, AFL-CIO, et al. v. NLRB* 1986:717).

Citing its own decision in *NLRB v. Apollo Tire*, the ninth circuit court argued that to deny undocumented workers backpay awards would encourage employers to hire and discriminate against undocumented workers. Pregerson noted that Justice O'Connor had arrived at a similar conclusion in *Sure-Tan*. Acknowledging that employers faced contempt charges if they violated an NLRB cease and desist order, Pregerson argued that the risk would be slight and thus not serve as an adequate deterrent to violations of the NLRA.

Contempt proceedings would require a further complaint from an undocumented employee who knew that filing a charge would immediately place his or her immigration status in jeopardy. Few undocumented workers would take such a chance. Moreover, the knowledge that deportation proceedings are a likely consequence of filing a successful unfair labor practice charge would chill severely the inclination of any unlawfully treated undocumented worker to vindicate his or her rights before the NLRB. (*Local 512, Warehouse and Office Workers' Union, ILGWU, AFL-CIO, et al. v. NLRB* 1986:719)

Thus, the condition of proof of legal status was inconsistent with the goals of the NLRA. "Indeed," Pregerson averred, "equalizing the backpay liability for unlawful acts against undocumented and American workers could deter employers from hiring undocumented workers and thus marginally reduce illegal entry to the United States" (*Local 512, Warehouse and Office Workers' Union, ILGWU, AFL-CIO, et al. v. NLRB* 1986:720). Judge Breezer, in a lengthy dissent, argued, as he had in *Bevles*, that the NLRB's decision to condition backpay on proof of legal immigration status was, in fact, mandated by *Sure-Tan*.[8]

Judge Pregerson noted that federal immigration laws were exceedingly complex. Neither possession of a green card nor lack of documentation are conclusive evidence of being in the country legally. Pregerson pointed out that there were thirty-three general categories of people who were not permitted to enter the United States, a myriad of circumstances that prevented people from being deported, and lengthy appeal processes. The ninth circuit court found it "hard to believe that Congress wished to place upon an NLRB compliance officer, probably untrained in the intricacies of immigration law, the responsibility of determining the alien status of an undocumented worker and denying that person the benefit of the NLRA's remedies" (*Local 512, Warehouse and Office Workers' Union, ILGWU, AFL-CIO, et al. v. NLRB* 1986:721).

An amicus brief submitted by the Mexican American Legal Defense and Educational Fund (MALDEF) and the National Center for Immigrants' Rights (NCIR) was particularly effective in laying out in a detailed fashion the complexity and intricacies of immigration laws and the considerable discretionary power in the hands of the attorney general. The brief by MALDEF and NCIR argued, essentially, what the ninth circuit court concluded: Determining an individual's immigration status was not a simple matter.

> It would . . . be wholly improper for the Board to circumscribe a remedy for unfair labor practices based on an employee's inability to produce immigration documents, thereby denying full remedies to some deportable workers, while allowing the same remedies to others who are equally deportable. This conclusion is compelled by both due process and equal protection. (Mexican American Legal Defense and Educational Fund 1985:20)

With reference specifically to the backpay award, the lawyers for these two organizations argued,

> An award of backpay to employees of indeterminate status presents no conflict between the NLRA and federal immigration policy. The purpose of backpay is to restore a discriminatee to the position he or she would have had before the unfair labor practice. By extending backpay awards to aggrieved employees, the Board would not be encouraging unlawful immigration into the United States, because undocumented workers are not motivated to come to this country in the belief that they may collect backpay for malfeasance committed by a prospective employer. On the other hand, denying relief to these employees could make them more vulnerable to employer exploitation and more attractive choices for employment. Without meaningful and enforceable remedies, employers would more likely hire undocumented workers as a means of circumventing federal and state labor laws. Employers could then use undocumented workers to destroy employee unity and cripple the rights of all employees to organize. (Mexican American Legal Defense and Educational Fund 1985:3–4)

While the remedy portion of the *Sure-Tan* decision was open to varying interpretations, the designation of undocumented workers as "employees" within the meaning of the NLRA was unambiguous (notwithstanding Justices William H. Rehnquist's and

Lewis F. Powell, Jr.'s dissent on this issue). But would undocumented immigrants continue to be protected by the NLRA with the passage of the Immigration Reform and Control Act of 1986? Justice O'Connor wrote in her opinion that since it was not illegal to hire undocumented immigrants, there was no reason to conclude that there was a conflict between the application of the NLRA and the INA. Did IRCA change this?

While workers, organizers, and several attorneys expressed to me concerns that in the post-IRCA period undocumented workers would no longer be considered "employees" under the NLRA, their worse fears have not been realized. Undocumented workers essentially have retained the protection of the NLRA against unfair labor practices by their employers. In *NLRB v. Ashkenazy Property Management Corporation* (1987), for example, the ninth circuit court ruled that remedies for violations of the NLRA should be implemented regardless of workers' citizenship status. This case straddled the IRCA.

In January 1981, L'Ermitage Hotel fired its housekeeping staff. On behalf of the workers, the Hotel Employees and Restaurant Employees and Bartenders Union, Local 11, filed an unfair labor practice charge against the employer, claiming that the workers had been fired for engaging in union activities. In April 1982, the ALJ found in favor of the workers and recommended that they be reinstated and receive backpay, with interest. The NLRB adopted the ALJ's order, but the hotel's owner refused to comply with it. The NLRB asked the ninth circuit court to enforce the order. The court affirmed the order and returned it to the board for compliance proceedings. In the interim, the IRCA was passed by Congress and signed by the President.

On December 19, 1986, the NLRB sent a letter to the workers who had been fired by the hotel, requiring that they show proof of residency in the United States since January 1, 1982, the legalization period under IRCA, as a condition to reinstatement or receiving backpay. Affected employees had until January 9, 1987, to respond. The workers were advised by their attorneys not to respond to the NLRB's request. Most did not. The case went before the ninth circuit court once more.

The workers argued that the NLRB's requirement violated their rights. The circuit court's previous decision did not require workers to prove that they were in the country legally. They cited *Felbro*, as well, for the proposition that the NLRB did not have either the authority or expertise to determine a person's immigration status. Finally, the workers' attorneys argued that it had not been Congress's intent to limit labor law (and other) protections undocumented immigrants enjoyed during the pre-IRCA period. The ninth circuit court rejected the employer's assertion that IRCA nullified *Felbro* and ordered the NLRB to hold compliance hearings — but without immigration status as an issue. The board complied, but the hotel persisted in its refusal to give undocumented immigrants backpay.

In September 1988, another ALJ recommended that the hotel be ordered to pay back wages of approximately $75,000 to the discharged workers. Again, the hotel refused to comply. An NLRB panel affirmed the ALJ's ruling. The hotel refused to comply and filed a Petition for Review in the United States Court of Appeals for the District of Columbia Circuit. In a brief on behalf of Local 11, the union alleged that the petitioners (L'Ermitage Hotel) were "forum shopping" by taking their case to yet another court and argued, as did the NLRB in its brief, that not a single judicial or board decision since *Felbro* had rejected the ninth circuit court's interpretation of *Sure-Tan* or its conclusion that Congress intended discriminatees to be entitled to all traditional NLRB remedies regardless of their immigration status. The union noted in its brief that in 1988 the second circuit court, in *Rios v. Enterprise Association of Steamfitters Local 638*, a Title VII case, adopted the ninth circuit court's analysis in *Felbro*, as did the eleventh circuit court the same year with reference to the FLSA (*Patel v. Quality Inn South* 1988).

In June 1988, the United States Court of Appeals for the Eleventh Circuit overturned a lower-court decision, *Patel v. Sumani*

Corp. (1987), in which Judge William M. Acker held that an undocumented immigrant could not enforce the minimum wage and overtime provisions of the FLSA. Rajni J. Patel, on a six-week visitor's visa from his native India, entered the United States on June 1, 1982. He remained in the country beyond the six-week period and in July 1983 moved into a room in the Quality Inn South, in Birmingham, Alabama. Patel claimed to have worked for the hotel through October 1985. In August 1986, Patel sued the Sumani Corporation, the owner of the hotel, for unpaid back wages in the amount of $47,132, claiming that the employer had violated the minimum wage and overtime provisions of the FLSA. The defendants denied that Patel had worked for them and argued that as an undocumented immigrant he had no claim under the FLSA.

Judge Acker requested and received from the United States Department of Labor (DOL) a statement on whether an undocumented immigrant could make a claim under the FLSA. The secretary of labor took the position that the right of an undocumented immigrant "to maintain an action" under the FLSA "seems clear." The department cited the ninth circuit court's interpretation of the *Sure-Tan* decision to note that undocumented immigrants were entitled to remedies. With the exception of one case (*In re Reyes* 1987), which the DOL brought to his attention over the telephone, Acker noted that the DOL cited no case and no legislative history to support its position. In *In re Reyes*, the fifth circuit court held that undocumented immigrants were protected by the FLSA.

Noting that the fifth circuit court arrived at its decision *"without citing a single authority"* [emphasis in original], Judge Acker concurred with Judge Edith Jones's dissent (*Patel v. Sumani Corp., Inc.* 1987:1529). Jones knew of no legal precedent for the court's decision, prompting Acker to ask, "Why are there no decided cases on this subject when there have undoubtedly been millions of illegal aliens employed in this country for years at less than minimum wage?" He then responded to his own question.

The logical reason is that no illegal alien ever entertained the thought he was entitled to invoke the FLSA until the recent era of amnesty, when Patel was emboldened to "come out of the closet," so to speak. It is difficult to think that since the FLSA was adopted years ago no lawyer has ever filed a suit on behalf of an employed illegal alien, that is, unless the multitalented and hungry legal profession unanimously shared the view of Judge Jones. (*Patel V. Sumani Corp., Inc.* 1987:1529–30)

He cited IRCA as another reason for siding with Judge Jones.

In rejecting Patel's right to any remedy under the FLSA, Judge Acker reasoned that "to interpret the protection of the FLSA to apply to illegal aliens would so obviously conflict with the purpose and policy behind the IRCA so as to fly in the face of what Congress has attempted to do" (*Patel v. Sumani Corp., Inc.* 1987:1531). He concluded that Patel was not an " 'individual' within the definition of an employee under the FLSA" and therefore had "no standing to complain of any violations of the FLSA" (*Patel v. Sumani Corp., Inc.* 1987:1531). His decision was based in substantial part on the fact that it was illegal to hire undocumented immigrants. The relationship between employer and undocumented employee to which Justice O'Connor had referred in *Sure-Tan* became illegal after November 6, 1986.

Judge Acker posited that undocumented workers took native workers' jobs and hurt the country's economy. Protecting them under the FLSA, he argued, would only encourage them to enter and work in the country illegally: "On the other hand, not allowing an illegal alien to enforce the wage and hour laws discourages such entry and has no detrimental effect on the employment of citizens and aliens legally admitted into the United States" (*Patel v. Sumani Corp., Inc.* 1987:1534). Furthermore, Acker reasoned, "there is no advantage or incentive for employers to prefer illegal aliens over legal resident workers," given the criminal and civil sanctions of the IRCA against employing undocumented immigrants (*Patel v. Sumani Corp., Inc.* 1987:1535). Acker assumed that the law would and could be enforced effectively. The International Ladies Garment Workers Union (ILGWU) appealed his ruling.

The United States Court of Appeals for the Eleventh Circuit reversed Acker's decision (*Patel v. Quality Inn South* 1988). Ruling that undocumented workers were protected under the FLSA, Judge Vance, writing for the court, noted that nothing in the legislative history of IRCA suggested that Congress intended to limit the rights of undocumented workers under the FLSA. This flew in the face of Acker's contention that Congress had intended otherwise. The following excerpt from a report on the IRCA by the House of Representatives Committee on Education and Labor is part of this legislative history.

> The committee does not intend that any provision of this Act would limit the power of State or Federal labor standards agencies such as Occupational Safety and Health Administration, the Wage and Hour Division of the Department of Labor, the Equal Employment Opportunity Commission, the National Labor Relations Board, or Labor arbitrators, in conformity with existing law, to remedy unfair practices committed against undocumented employees for exercising their rights before such agencies or for engaging in activities protected by these agencies. To do otherwise would be counter-productive of our intent to limit the hiring of undocumented employees and the depressing effect on working conditions caused by their employment. (U.S. Congress. H.R. 99–682, part 2, 1986)

The following portion of a House Judiciary Committee report also leaves little doubt as to Congress's intent.

> It is not the intention of the Committee that the employer sanctions provisions of the bill be used to undermine or diminish in any way labor protections in existing law, or to limit the powers of federal or state labor relations boards, labor standards agencies, or labor arbitrators to remedy unfair practices committed against undocumented employees for exercising their

rights before such agencies or for engaging in activities protected by existing law. In particular, the employer sanctions provisions are not intended to limit in any way the scope of the term "employee" in Section 2(3) of the National Labor Relations Act (NLRA), as amended, or of the rights and protections stated in Sections 7 and 8 of that Act. As the Supreme Court observed in *Sure-Tan Inc. v. NLRB*, 467 U.S. 883 (1984) application of the NLRA "helps to assure that the wages and employment conditions of lawful residents are not adversely affected by the competition of illegal alien employees who are not subject to the standard terms of employment" 467 U.S. at 893. (U.S. Congress. H.R. 99–682, part 2. 1986)

Judge Vance noted that section 111(d) of the IRCA was even more revealing. Congress had earmarked funds for the enforcement of the FLSA on behalf of undocumented workers. This provision of the IRCA, quoted by Vance in his written opinion, reads,

There are authorized to be appropriated, in addition to such sums as may be available for such purposes, such sums as may be necessary to the Department of Labor for enforcement activities of the Wage and Hour Division . . . in order to deter the employment of unauthorized aliens and remove the economic incentive for employers to exploit and use such aliens. (*Patel v. Quality Inn South* 1988:704)

Both the act's legislative history and this section of the IRCA suggest rather strongly that it was Congress's intent to include undocumented immigrants under the FLSA umbrella.

The eleventh circuit court also ruled that there was nothing in the FLSA to suggest that undocumented workers are not entitled to the same remedies as all other workers. Moreover, the court argued that "by reducing the incentive to hire such workers the FLSA's coverage of undocumented aliens helps to discourage illegal immigration and is thus fully consistent with the objectives of the IRCA" (*Patel v. Quality Inn South* 1988:704–5). Without FLSA protections, these workers would be even more attractive to employers. Vance doubted, and correctly so, that undocumented immigrants were attracted to the United States by the protection of its labor laws. In fact, the workers in Camagua did not know that they were protected by the NLRA and FLSA until the union told them.

Undocumented immigrants who have filed unfair labor practice charges against their employer typically have been members of unions or workers trying to unionize. The vast majority of undocumented immigrants do not belong to unions, do not know someone who is or has been a union member, and have relatively little knowledge about unions and labor laws in the United States or their country of origin. Whether they are or are not protected by the country's labor laws is not an important factor, if a factor at all, in their decision to emigrate to the United States.

With reference to the Department of Labor's (DOL) position, rejected by Acker, Vance noted in his decision that while they were not bound by the DOL's interpretation, the DOL was entitled to "considerable deference" as the agency charged with the act's implementation. Since the World War II, the DOL had, on numerous occasions, enforced the FLSA on behalf of undocumented immigrants, following the wage and hour administrator's decision in 1942 that alien prisoners of war were entitled to be paid the minimum wage since they were covered by the FLSA (*Patel v. Quality Inn South* 1988:703). The Equal Employment Opportunity Commission (EEOC) also filed an amicus brief stating that it did not distinguish between documented and undocumented aliens in determining eligibility for remedial orders under Title VII.

In arriving at its decision that undocumented workers were "employees" under the FLSA, the eleventh circuit court referred to section 203(e) of the act where "employee" was defined to include "any individual employed by an employer." The FLSA also listed exceptions, but undocumented immigrants were not on the list. Vance offered the FLSA's legislative history as evidence of Congress's intent to define employee broadly and the Supreme

Court's consistent refusal to exempt from FLSA coverage anyone not excepted by the act. With reference to the NLRA, as indicated earlier, the Supreme Court was even clearer when it wrote that "since undocumented aliens are not among the few groups of workers expressly exempted by Congress, they plainly come within the broad statutory definition of 'employee'" (*Sure-Tan, Inc., v. NLRB* 1984:743). During oral argument, in fact, the defendants conceded that nothing in the FLSA or its legislative history indicated that Congress intended to exclude undocumented immigrants.

The defendants' principal argument was that IRCA, in effect, changed everything. Because of IRCA, the defendants contended, undocumented immigrants were no longer protected by the FLSA. But even if they were, Quality Inn South argued, the justices in the *Sure-Tan* decision had precluded them from recovering damages. In rejecting this contention, Judge Vance pointed to IRCA's legislative history, the act itself, and relevant case law. With reference to the issue of remedy, Judge Vance first observed that nowhere did the FLSA limit the remedies available to any of the workers covered by the act. Judge Vance reasoned that the question presented before him was a different one from the one answered by the Supreme Court in *Sure-Tan*. Patel, he noted, was trying to recover backpay for work he had performed. "Under these circumstances," Judge Vance wrote, "the rationale the Supreme Court used in *Sure-Tan* to limit the availability of back pay under the NLRA to periods when the employee was lawfully present in the United States is inapplicable" (*Patel v. Quality Inn South* 1988:705–6).[9] Judge Vance concluded that Patel was entitled to remedies, regardless of his immigration status.

Despite the *Felbro* and *Ashkenazy* decisions, on October 27, 1987, the NLRB's general counsel, Rosemary Collyer, sent a chill through the ranks of organizers of undocumented workers when she issued a memorandum instructing NLRB staff to condition backpay and reinstatement on proof of citizenship or temporary resident status. She withdrew the memo five months later, however, and released a new memo in September 1988 that superseded all previous memos on the subject (Collyer 1988a).[10] Noting that only the INS can decide whether an immigrant is living and working in the United States lawfully, Collyer concluded — to the relief of many organizers and unionside labor attorneys — that the immigration status of an individual terminated by his or her employer should not be addressed in litigation before the board.

> Proceedings before the Board, including settlement efforts, should not be held in abeyance pending the outcome of any INS proceeding to determine immigration status. A discriminatee is entitled to reinstatement and backpay unless and until the INS rules that the discriminatee is not entitled to be present and employed in the U.S. For, until the INS determines that an individual is not lawfully entitled to be present and employed in the U.S., a Board order requiring reinstatement and backpay does not conflict with immigration law or policy. (Collyer 1988b:2–3)

Grandfathered discriminatees, that is, employees hired before November 6, 1986, who had not been proven by an employer to be working without documents, would be entitled to the normal remedies of reinstatement and backpay. This was the case even if the grandfathered worker had not applied for lawful status under IRCA or other provision of the INA. In other words, the burden of proof that the discriminatee was in the country illegally fell on the employer. Furthermore, since an individual could conceivably qualify to be present and employed under another provision of immigration laws, the discriminatee's failure to receive temporary resident status under IRCA would not satisfy the employer's burden of proof (Collyer 1988b:3–5).

Citing the Supreme Court's decision in *Sure-Tan*, the board's general counsel averred that in the event that a discriminatee was determined by the INS not to be in the country legally, the board would not seek reinstatement. The discriminatee would be entitled to backpay for the period prior to the INS ruling, however, if he or she had been in the United States and available for work during this period (Collyer 1988b:5). This issue had been left unresolved in *Sure-Tan* (1984), but in *INS v. Adan López-Mendoza et al.* (1984), Collyer noted, the Supreme Court indicated that "retrospective sanctions . . . may be imposed against an employer by the NLRB for unfair labor practices involving illegal aliens. Moreover, backpay for such a period is appropriate because it should be presumed that a discriminatee is lawfully present and entitled to work until the contrary is shown" (Collyer 1988b:5). Retrospective sanctions, Collyer presumed, referred to backpay. She reasoned, moreover, that an immigrant is presumed to be in the country legally until proven otherwise. Even if the discriminatee is determined by the INS to be in the country illegally, this determination applies only from the time of the ruling forward. Thus, he or she would be entitled to backpay until the date of the INS ruling (Collyer 1988b:5). Employees hired after November 6, 1986, fared very differently.

With the passage of IRCA, employers were required to get a completed I-9 form from any employee hired after November 6, 1986, and to fill out their portion of the form.[11] Failure to comply could result in criminal sanctions. As a consequence, if a discriminatee refused to complete the form, he or she would not be entitled to reinstatement or backpay "for subsequent periods" (Collyer 1988b:6). Collyer acknowledged in her memo that the legislative history of IRCA indicated that the act was not intended to limit the NLRB's power to order reinstatement and backpay to undocumented workers. Collyer argued, however, that it was *Sure-Tan* and not IRCA that limited the power of the NLRB in such cases. Backpay would be sought for an individual for the period during which he or she could meet the I-9 requirements. In cases involving other forms of discrimination (for example, reduction of pay), however, backpay could be available "even if the employee has been adjudicated to be an undocumented alien" (Collyer 1988b:7).

In ruling as he did in *Patel v. Sumani,* Judge Acker reasoned that immigrants would be discouraged from seeking employment in the United States if they were denied the legal protections of the FLSA. He failed to consider a much more likely scenario, which the eleventh circuit court envisioned: undocumented workers being forced further underground and becoming even more susceptible to exploitation and control by employers *and* less accessible to unions. Substantively, while labor law protections do not affect the decision to emigrate, they do affect decisions to organize.

Future court and NLRB decisions and enforcement of the NLRA and FLSA will certainly be critical, as they have always been, in defining the battlefield for the struggle between labor and management. The courts and the NLRB can make it difficult for employers to discriminate against undocumented workers by protecting them against unfair labor practices. On the other hand, by stripping away the labor law protections to which undocumented workers have been entitled to the present, they will leave workers at the mercy of unscrupulous employers. And since undocumented immigration shows little sign of waning appreciably, many employers will continue to hire workers from the undocumented pool — increasingly on their terms and to the detriment of undocumented *and* native workers.

Chapter V

Undocumented Workers and Organized Labor

While the assertion that undocumented immigrants are unorganizable is understandable, given the tendency to focus on their legal vulnerability, the analysis presented here suggests otherwise. This study, a deviant case analysis of a firm in which undocumented workers voted for union representation and signed a collective bargaining agreement with their employer, examined the effects of undocumented status on the unionization of immigrant workers from Mexico and Central America and found that under certain conditions undocumented workers organize to protest and improve their conditions of work.

First, the presumed paralyzing fear of deportation is diluted by the rather inconspicuous presence of the INS in Los Angeles and the relative ease of returning in the event of apprehension and deportation. This is not to minimize the risks and costs involved. Migrants have been robbed; some, crossing dark highways in an attempt to stay with the rest of the group, have been killed by cars.

Second, the distinction between short-term and long-term residents made by organizers and some scholars is a critical one in understanding the unionization of undocumented workers. Simply stated, permanent settlers, or long-term residents, are easier to organize than temporary migrants, or short-term residents. Significantly, the former has been growing ever larger in size since the 1960s.

Immigrants, and especially long-term residents, are plugged into social networks that provide them with valuable and potentially empowering information on where to live and work, how to find employment, what to expect from employers — in short, how to navigate the city. "Although legal vulnerability undoubtedly influences the search for employment and the willingness to bargain for higher wages, the strength of this effect depends on the information available to the immigrant" (Bailey 1987:132). While short-term residents and recently arrived migrants are connected to social networks, longer-term residents' networks tend to be more extensive and varied.

Third, the length of time in the interior tends to alter immigrants' frame of reference. Initially satisfied that they are making more money than they made back home, they eventually begin to compare their wages, conditions of work, material possessions, and quality of life more generally to others in Los Angeles who are similarly employed. In some instances and under certain conditions, such comparisons spur efforts to improve their situation. One way to do this, especially if other avenues are closed to them, is to unionize, as the majority of Camagua's workers opted to do.

Another factor mitigating the fear of deportation is the unique occupational niche filled by immigrant workers in the Los Angeles economy. The perception, one supported in some measure by the data, that certain jobs "belong" to them is reassuring and contributes significantly to a sense of security expressed by Camagua's workers, and by workers from other firms. Contributing as well to this sense of security has been unions' increasing interest in organizing immigrant workers, irrespective of legal status, and the fact that undocumented workers have been deemed "employees" under the NLRA by the courts and, thereby, protected by national labor laws.

In the Camagua case, the breakdown of paternalistic ties between the owner and workers and the poor transition from a simple to a more complex system of labor control required by rapid economic growth, also helped to ripen the company for unionization. Finally, the union's ability to capitalize on the weakened

personal ties between the owner and his employees, and its determination and substantial commitment of resources to organize
Camagua, were key to the successful unionization of the firm.

My findings do not necessarily dispute the assertion that "as
long as illegals are vulnerable to deportation, they will be ultimately impossible to organize into viable unions" (Jenkins
1978:530). But just how vulnerable were Camagua's workers to
deportation? While it is a fact that undocumented immigrants can
be apprehended and deported (and in this respect are clearly
vulnerable), the probability of being apprehended in Los Angeles
and other points north of the San Clemente checkpoint is so
low and the significance of the other mitigating factors discussed
in this book so high that the vulnerability—both real and perceived—of immigrants to deportation is substantially reduced. In
the process, so is their fear of being arrested and deported by the
INS. The difficulty in organizing undocumented immigrants is
explained not so much by their legal status as by the factors that
make it difficult to organize *any* worker—native or immigrant,
documented or undocumented—in most industries and sectors of
a declining national economy.

While this is a case study of one organizing campaign, the implications, both theoretical and practical, are broader. The idea that
undocumented status prevents the organization of these workers
suggests a structural set of factors that has been questioned by
some scholars. Bodnar (1982:9) concludes from his study on industrial workers in the early part of the century that "historians have
readily portrayed them as victims whose behavior and thought are
shaped by external forces such as technological determinism, management initiatives, or even political and state action." The same
determinism is evident in discussions of undocumented workers.
The world of Camagua's workers and their contemporaries, like
the world of their European counterparts at the turn of the twentieth century, is a complex one "grounded not only in the workplace, but also in intricate networks of family, communal, and
work associations" (Bodnar 1982:166). It was to this larger world

that the "consciousness and behavior" of these workers — and Camagua's — were tied.

Human beings are not simply acted upon. They act back, and undocumented workers, despite the constraints of their undocumented status, are no exception. Typically, human beings are knowledgeable about the conditions in which they are operating and of the consequences of their actions; and they can describe, discursively, why they acted as they did (Giddens 1984). Camagua's workers demonstrated this.

The rationality (or irrationality) of human behavior has been and continues to be a central question for social movements scholars. Attributing rationality to individuals' decisions to participate in collective action is a radical departure from earlier social-psychological theories. In the case of Camagua's workers, to be undocumented and yet openly, even militantly, participate in a union campaign seems irrational. But is it any more irrational than decisions by native workers to organize despite the very real prospect of job loss?

What the interviews reveal clearly is the rational manner in which workers chose to support, or not to support, unionization. The fear of deportation, in fact, was not a particularly rational one for undocumented immigrants who were long-time residents of Los Angeles, with families and roots in their home and work communities. The union, in turn, fortified the perception of security by providing workers with an organization, legal assistance, and the assurance that they were protected by the country's labor laws.

The phenomenological approach I employed allowed me to probe the issue of undocumented status as it shaped the world views of the immigrants themselves. I attempted to reconstruct their world as they saw it. The approach also allowed me to establish the level of trust needed to get workers to talk freely about their experiences as immigrants and workers and permitted me to explore more easily and in greater depth important social-psychological factors bearing on the unionization of undocumented immigrants. A social-psychological approach to social movements does a good job of linking "structural conditions, articulated demands, and personal participation" (Ferree and Miller 1985:43).

The need to incorporate social-psychological variables into social-movement theory has been urged by numerous researchers, in part because they reveal "processes of social-movement participation on the individual level" (Klandermans 1984:584). Analyzing the interaction between individuals is theoretically important. The importance of this "psychological truism" is that an individual's decision to participate in a movement is based on the perceived costs and benefits (Klandermans 1984). This applies both to joining a movement and becoming an active participant.

Zurcher and Snow's (1981) analytical distinction between the "recruitment process" and "commitment-building and conversion processes" is reflected in the following comment by Rivas: "It's easy to get them, but much harder to keep them." For any movement to succeed it must be able to convert recruits into committed participants. While the type and depth of commitments may vary, there must be a core of activists willing to perform the necessary, often time-consuming and unpleasant, tasks in any organizing campaign.

At Camagua, the poor treatment accorded the company's employees by supervisors, perhaps more than any other issue, sustained workers' commitment. While Camagua's workers rationally calculated whether or not to participate, their participation cannot be understood fully without recognizing their "feeling states." Believing that they would win concessions, many of them were prepared to come up empty handed, collectively or personally.

Neither individuals nor organizations have access to all the information they need regarding the costs and benefits of their participation (Zurcher and Snow 1981). Even if they did, people do not always act in a self-interested manner. In their critique of Olson (1977), Fireman and Gamson (1988:9) contend that usually it is not selective incentives that motivate people to engage in collective action; it is organizers (and events) that "build solidarity, raise consciousness of common interests, and create opportunities for collective action."

Some social-movement scholars criticize the incentive model employed by resource mobilization theorists for failing to adequately explain how individuals are mobilized. "Costs and benefits certainly play a role in generating movement support, but the translation of objective social relationships into subjectively experienced group interests is also critical in building movements, as in political activity generally" (Ferree and Miller 1985:39). At Camagua, selective incentives played a role in the union campaign. On one occasion, for example, the union paid the sewers, the most skilled of Camagua's workers, not to come in. Some of the workers, undoubtedly, were involved (or not involved) because of self-interest. Free-riders (Olson 1977) were plentiful on both sides. Yet, in the end, the workers who sacrificed the most and worked the hardest urged others to accept the contract despite the company's refusal to reinstate them.

A majority of the workers did not want to accept the final contract offer without the reinstatement of their fellow workers who had been fired by the company. Victor Casas, one of the workers who had been fired by Ramírez and had been very active in the boycott, urged the others to vote in favor of the contract. Cecilia Durán recalled this meeting in which the workers voted and Casas exhorted his former coworkers to accept the contract: "Victor said, '*Compañeros*, if it means sacrificing our job, at least we know we got a contract. We got a union contract. It's a bad one, but we got our contract. We made him sign.' It was the most beautiful thing. Everybody was crying." Other workers who had been fired by Ramírez joined Casas in urging acceptance of the contract. Clearly, people can and do act on the "basis of principle or moral considerations" (Zurcher and Snow 1981:469).

The importance of emotion and passion in collective action often is not adequately appreciated in social-movement research (Perrow 1988; Zurcher and Snow 1981). In the case of Camagua, workers' passions and emotions were stirred and tapped by the union in meetings, rallies, and other group activities. The struggle was personalized and affected the behavior of the owner, the workers, the organizers. Felipe Hernández, a truck driver, told me that he did not care if the contract was a good one or not. "That son-of-a-bitch [Bob Ramírez] was going to sign a contract!" Hernández insisted.

Organization, however, is crucial to the type of protest that occurred at Camagua. However important passion and emotions are, the union provided experience, legal assistance, contacts, telephones, transportation, and other organizational capabilities so vital to the success of any organizing campaign. The corporate campaign was well organized and the union relied on an assortment of preexisting community organizations to apply pressure on Ramírez. The social networks in which workers were enmeshed were key resources as well. But organization alone is not enough. "The problem is not organization per se, but organizations that fail to develop and maintain a sense of enthusiasm and anticipation" (Zurcher and Snow 1981:478).[1] The success of the Camagua organizing campaign depended on both organization and passion. In the process, an empowering "culture of solidarity" emerged (Fantasia 1988).[2]

This culture of solidarity emerges from social conflict through which "new values are incubated, new forms of activity generated, and an associational bond of a new type formed" (Fantasia 1988:174).[3] Union activists in the Camagua campaign, many of them members of the negotiating committee and the workers conducting the boycott, "thought of themselves as a collective entity that embodied a certain vision distinguishing them from others and representing a new approach to authority, hierarchy, and relations to one another" (Fantasia 1988:174). Many workers were changed, perhaps forever, by the experience.

Social psychology can tell us a great deal about the microprocesses of mobilization (Gamson, Fireman, and Rytina 1982). To study such micromobilization, Gamson, Fireman, and Rytina (1982:14–17) suggest focusing on "encounters with authorities" to examine "long-term mobilization processes," three of which are evident in my own research: (1) fashioning an alternative belief system supporting collective action, (2) breaking the bonds of authority, and (3) organizing a challenge.[4] In the Camagua case, workers managed to redefine a situation that previously had seemed natural to them. The rapid growth of the plant and the breakdown of paternalistic ties provided an opening for the redefinition of the situation. The union, in turn, played an important role in helping workers to see "that the unimpeded operation of the authority system, on this occasion, would result in an injustice" (Gamson, Fireman, Rytina 1982:14–15).

Both supporters and detractors of a movement can (and often do) affect this perceived reality. Clearly, this was the case in the Camagua campaign, but here the company's influence was relatively ineffectual.[5] Persuasion is an important factor, and the union (particularly Néstor Rivas) was especially adept at persuading workers to turn to the union to seek redress of their grievances (Klandermans 1984).

Barrington Moore (1978) and Doug McAdam (1983) argue convincingly that insurgency requires the aggrieved to redefine their situation as an unjust and mutable one. This is a difficult process.

> Normally . . . such definitions of social injustice are blocked or cannot be converted into collective images. Past experiences of failed insurgency, elite control of information and socialization processes, disorganization and lack of "free spaces" for creating alternative definitions of reality, and simple psychological adaptation to the state of powerlessness create quiescent attitudes among the excluded toward their objective deprivations. (Jenkins 1985:5)

Furthermore,

> The consciousness of excluded groups is dual. . . . An insurgent consciousness based on a sense of social injustice coexists along-

side a contradictory deferential consciousness that highlights the "fairness" and immutability of the prevailing order. These contradictory belief systems coexist and, because of the dominance of elites and the powerlessness of the excluded, the former becomes private while the latter is public knowledge. The result is the political passivity of the excluded. (Jenkins 1985:6)

But the excluded do not always remain passive. The notion of ideological hegemony and its "related concepts of false-consciousness, mystification, and ideological state apparatuses" can be misleading in understanding class relations and class conflict. "The concept of hegemony ignores the extent to which most subordinate classes are able, on the basis of their daily material experience, to penetrate and demystify the prevailing ideology" (Scott 1985:317). While the majority of Camagua's workers may not have seen through the prevailing ideology completely, many did so sufficiently to mount a successful challenge.

Several developments weakened the company's position, strengthened that of the workers, and exposed certain inequities more clearly. The company failed to adapt quickly enough to its rapid expansion. Ill-trained and abusive supervisors and the growing distance between the owner and his workers (created by the rapid growth of the company) undermined the paternalistic relationship Ramírez had cultivated, which had served him well over the years. The union played an important role in a number of ways. While discontents predated the appearance of Amaro at the plant gates in 1984, the union helped to define their grievances more precisely and convert them into purposeful action.[6]

Trying to make sense of the Camagua organizing campaign by focusing on solely sociological or solely psychological factors would result in a "truncated" understanding of what occurred, as it would in the analysis of any social movement (Zurcher and Snow 1981). The demand for these workers' labor in certain industries and jobs, the relatively minor threat of apprehension by the INS in Los Angeles, the immigrant workers' roots and social networks in the city, the resources invested by the union, and the labor laws protecting undocumented workers were important structural conditions indispensable to the workers' losing their fear of the INS and Camagua's becoming a union shop. Yet the unionization of the plant would not have occurred had a culture of solidarity not developed and had many workers not made personal sacrifices, placing the collective good over their own personal good. The deterioration of the relationship between Ramírez and his employees, a relationship he depended on to get maximum production and loyalty from his workers, contributed as well to the unionization of the firm. On a very personal level many workers felt betrayed by Ramírez and were motivated to unionize by the indignities they refused to suffer any longer from abusive supervisors.

The tendency has been to define undocumented status too narrowly. Why should we be surprised, for example, to find that, on occasion, undocumented workers participate actively, and even militantly, in unionizing campaigns and contract negotiations? If undocumented status meant a high probability of being apprehended in the interior, no legal (including labor law) protections, the criminalization of and aggressive enforcement of laws against hiring undocumented workers, and stepped-up efforts to control the border, then we should be surprised. Prior to the passage of the IRCA in 1986, however, undocumented status in Los Angeles did not mean any of these things. It still seems not to. Moreover, for long-term immigrant residents of Los Angeles County, undocumented status does not mean isolation, lack of information, or fear of apprehension by the "migra," all factors that would make these workers more vulnerable and more difficult to organize.

The findings of this study suggest that immigration status will have an adverse effect on the organizability of undocumented workers under certain, but not all, conditions. First, if undocumented workers are no longer protected by the country's labor laws, they will be more vulnerable to unscrupulous employers. Second, if IRCA, and particularly the employer sanctions provision of the law, is enforced more aggressively, and the penalties for employers who violate the law are made considerably more severe, it will become much more difficult for undocumented workers to find work or remain with a firm for an extended and uninterrupted period of time. Third, if organized labor turns its back on these workers or simply fails to organize them aggressively, undocumented workers will be robbed of the organization and resources they need to demand fair wages, decent working conditions, and humane treatment by their employers. In each case the way in which these policy matters are resolved will have profound consequences not only for the undocumented, but for the native population as well.

In the preceding chapter, I discussed the first of these conditions in some detail. Undocumented workers continue to be protected by the country's labor laws. In 1991, the Supreme Court refused to hear L'Ermitage Hotel's appeal of the ninth circuit court's 1987 *NLRB v. Ashkenazy Property Management Corporation* decision. This was good news to immigrant workers, because the Court's action suggests that a majority of the justices accept lower-court interpretations of their ruling in *Sure-Tan Inc. v. NLRB* (1984). Denying undocumented workers labor law protections would make them more difficult to organize, but would have virtually no impact on the flow of undocumented immigrants into the country. The IRCA itself has had little, if any, impact on such immigration.

While the IRCA appeared to reduce the number of immigrants entering the country without documents during the first year, the law no longer seems to be deterring undocumented immigration from Mexico and Central America. "Clearly, we have reached the end of the period of fear, uncertainty, and confusion about the 1986 law, among workers still based in Mexico" (Cornelius 1988:1). Researchers from El Colegio de la Frontera Norte (COLEF) in Tijuana have concluded the same, based on their systematic observations of the most heavily traveled route along the border since the passage of the new law.

Following passage of the IRCA, workers reported threats by

employers. Some employers began telling workers that under the new law they were taking a risk by hiring them. They told their undocumented workers that without documents they would not be able to find another job. Mario Santana, a striking worker in a dye plant, recalled being told by an employer, "If I fire you, you're going to have a difficult time finding another job. So be thankful that you have one." Ramírez himself, a critic of employer sanctions, remarked,

> On the other side of the coin, none of my employees want to leave their job or get fired. If they leave now, they can't get a job anywhere else because employers are asking for proof. I don't have to ask guys that are working for me now. The law doesn't begin until April. That's on the positive side. Guys who had been sons of bitches are all of a sudden nice guys.

There were reports by organizers and workers that when workers dared to ask for a raise, the owner asked them for documents, including those who had been hired prior to November 6, 1986.[7] Some employers immediately began to cut wages and lower piece rates. These tactics were directed particularly at grandfathered workers and recent arrivals. These threats and tactics, however, appeared to be the exception.

It remains to be seen if stricter enforcement of employer sanctions and well-publicized criminal prosecutions of immigrants using fraudulent documents will reduce significantly the flow of undocumented immigrants. Undocumented immigrants continue to find work in southern California, often using fraudulent documents. The bogus-documents industry received a shot in the arm from IRCA and is flourishing in southern California.[8] Moreover, the law penalizes only those employers who knowingly hire workers with falsified papers. Carlos Benavides, an administrator in an employment agency providing firms in Los Angeles County with workers, told me that they ask workers for documents, "but we're not experts on what is or is not a fraudulent document."

In response to employers' concerns about the authenticity of documents, Josie González (1988:113), an immigration attorney, advises them that "unless the picture is on upside down or crooked, or the card is still wet from the printing press, they should not try to be document examiners." González's main concern, she claims, is that her clients will scrutinize some documents more than others and thereby run the risk of a discrimination charge. She constantly reminds employers that they cannot insist on additional documents unless the ones provided do not appear to be genuine. She is also concerned that some employers will violate the law by refusing to hire an individual with a temporary grant of work authorization because the employer prefers not to invest time, money, and training in someone who may not be with the company for very long.

Some employers have expressed concerns about issues of equity in the enforcement of the law, fearing that their competitors might continue to hire undocumented workers while they comply with the law.[9] As Victor Pellot, an employer of undocumented workers in the bedding industry, commented,

> It's not that I like to work with illegals or the lower end of the spectrum of employees. But my philosophy is that I want to get whatever it is that puts my product together as inexpensively or as cheaply as my competitor. I don't want my competitor to have an edge on me. If I can have an edge on him, fine. As long as things are equal, that's fine too. If they close the border, that doesn't bother me.

Asked if he would break the law if his competitors continued to hire undocumented workers, he responded, "Yeah, that's right! Why should I give him an edge? He's going to undercut my price, and I'm following the rules and he's not? Who's going to win?"

The effects of enforcing IRCA much more strictly are difficult to predict, but a couple of potential scenarios are worth considering. While some businesses may raise wages and provide other incentives to attract native workers, others will have to close down or, if they have the capital, the inclination, and the type of business that can be transplanted, they may take their operations abroad in search of cheap labor. This could have a deleterious effect on local, state, and national economies. Moreover, there remains the matter of what it would take for many of the jobs performed currently by undocumented immigrants to be converted into jobs native workers will take willingly. Another scenario is a continuation of the status quo, but with workers driven further underground and rendered more vulnerable to exploitation by employers. The majority of the organizers predicted that IRCA would be amended to ease the pressure on employers. In fact, legislation to repeal the employer sanctions provisions of IRCA was introduced in both houses of Congress, fueled partly by the General Accounting Office's (GAO) March 29, 1990, third-year report that Latino and Asian citizens were being discriminated against as a consequence of the new law.

Purportedly an attempt to "regain control of the border," IRCA, wittingly or not, may have weakened the bargaining position of undocumented workers. By making it a crime to hire undocumented immigrants and more severely punishing illegal entry into the country, lawmakers claimed they could curtail dramatically, if not eliminate completely, undocumented immigration. Nearly six years after President Reagan signed this amendment into law, the flow of undocumented immigrants into the United States remains relatively unchanged. It has been labeled as an employer sanction bill by many politicians and the media, but a workers sanction label may be more appropriate. What do these changes portend for organized labor?

The labor movement in the United States is attempting a difficult comeback. "Over the past decade American unions have suffered defeat, demoralization, and decay" (Edwards and Podgursky 1986:14).[10] Unions have been winning fewer and fewer elections (70 percent of all NLRB elections in the 1950s and 45 percent in the 1980s) and making more and more concessions to management (Galenson 1986). "The autoworkers (UAW), steelworkers, and teamsters, all strong and well-entrenched unions, have over the past few years given back scheduled pay raises and cost-of-living adjustments" (Edwards and Podgursky 1986:15). Therefore, even if predictions about labor's impending demise are premature, as some stalwarts maintain, there is little question that labor is in trouble.

The following assessment by Freeman and Medoff (1984:244) focuses attention not only on the state's role, but also on the challenge facing organized labor to organize unorganized sectors of the labor force: "If unionism is to grow in the future, history suggests that the growth will occur suddenly, among groups new to unionism in a legal setting supportive of the collective organization of workers." While acknowledging the significance of employer opposition and public policies favorable to employers, Goldfield (1987) derides organized labor for its failure to be more aggressive in organizing workers in the private sector.

Marshall Gans's findings in California (discussed in Kuttner 1987) tend to confirm Goldfield's contention. Gans interviewed over 100 union officials and found that only 180 paid organizers, or 2.4 percent of their entire staffs, were in the field. Of these, only 96 were organizing 6.75 million unorganized private-sector workers. One labor expert estimates that if unions organized one-third of the workers expressing a desire to unionize, they would double their ranks (Kochan 1979). "It is most likely that union gains and large-scale growth in union membership will only be won in the foreseeable future on the basis of broad class struggle and innovative disruptions of production" (Goldfield 1987:243).

Significant shifts in the economy and changes in the character of the work force are likely to compel organized labor to focus much more on organizing workers in the secondary labor market, where immigrant workers (both documented and undocumented) constitute a substantial portion of the work force in some parts of the country, such as southern California, especially Los Angeles. Moreover, Latinos, blacks, and women make up a growing proportion of the work force, but in sectors of the economy in which organizing is difficult. Some studies, however, indicate that these groups are, by and large, receptive to unionization (Kistler 1979, 1984; Roberts 1984).

While trade unions have not been very successful in organizing workers in the secondary sector since World War II, my research suggests that the concentration of immigrant workers in secondary labor market firms and jobs does not explain organized labor's poor showing in this sector of the economy. Undocumented workers seem to be neither more nor less organizable because of their citizenship status than other workers in the secondary sector. Immigrant workers certainly have acted (and continue to act) as strikebreakers, but so have members of virtually every group in the country. A 1983 Greyhound strike, which saw twenty thousand people apply for strikers' jobs, should help dismiss any notion that undocumented immigrants have cornered the replacement worker market, just as blacks were accused of doing decades earlier (Freedman 1985:151). In the case of African-Americans, for example, unions often left them without any other choice by failing to organize them or by discriminating against them (Foner 1981).

The charge that eastern and southern European immigrants were unreceptive to unionization or made poor union members has also been made — and has been challenged by a number of labor historians (Cummings 1983; Fenton 1975; Hourwich 1912). Several of these historians place the blame for these immigrants' late and slow entry into unions largely on organized labor's restrictive policies. The argument that these immigrants were not very receptive to unionization, "ignores the patterns of exclusion which prevented many immigrants from union membership" and "enjoys limited empirical support as well" (Cummings 1983:31).

The CWU's serious commitment to organize Camagua, reflected in the resources poured into the campaign and the personal commitment of the organizers, was a necessary condition for the unionization of the firm. My findings suggest that Goldfield's (1987), Kuttner's (1987), and Gans's (in Kuttner 1987) assessments are correct, namely, that the labor movement must reorder its priorities and devote considerably more resources and energy to organizing the unorganized, among whom are immigrant workers. Many organizers in Los Angeles have recognized this, as reflected in the following statement by Elías Dávila, the president of a militant Los Angeles local:

> Many thousands of workers came to this country in search of better living conditions and because of the need to feed their families, leaving behind poverty which is partly created by the same U.S. corporations that undermine our working conditions and living standards. It is not our concern as workers whether they are here legally or illegally; our concern must be that all workers in this country have available all the protections to which they are entitled.

This statement indicates as well the global nature of the problem, one that organized labor cannot ignore.

In his assessment of undocumented immigration, Richard Rothstein (1986), a former organizer and now researcher and writer on labor issues, noted correctly the connection between United States foreign policy and immigration: "If we were not fomenting and financing their civil wars, Central Americans would not be fleeing here by the tens of thousands; in many local manufacturing plants, Salvadorans now outnumber Mexicans." Along the same lines, Delgado (1983:26) writes,

> The advancement of capital into the third world, coupled with U.S. military and political support for right-wing regimes, has had a twofold effect. First, this penetration has meant increased appropriation of the land and dispossession of the peasantry, forcing campesinos into other occupations or into the migratory stream of agricultural labor. Second, people in opposition to U.S.-supported repressive governments (as in the case of both El Salvador and Haiti) have been forced to seek political and economic refuge outside of their home countries, frequently in the United States.[11]

In the following excerpt from a report she prepared for the American Friends Service Committee (AFSC), Margaret Uglow (circa

1986–87) questions the sagacity, in some circles, of regarding the system as a closed one, bound by borders.

> The flow of money, trade, military materials, advertising abroad, national security activities, and investment constitutes constant, pervasive activity outside those borders which, over a period of many decades, has been nurturing the American way of life, its jobs, resources, and standards. . . . International activities and policies which have been assumed to be in the national interest of the United States have been in fact heavy contributors to, or at least essential conditions for, the massive exodus of peoples from their countries, particularly in this hemisphere.[12]

United States foreign policy, including military interventions, and the activities of multinationals in sending countries, such as Mexico and El Salvador, have contributed to the large influx of undocumented immigrants across the southern border, and organized labor has participated both directly and indirectly in the process.

The AFL-CIO has played an active role in establishing or supporting pliant unions in third world countries and undermining militant unions, mainly, in recent times, through its American Institute for Free Labor Development (AIFLD). According to the confidential minutes of the Labor Advisory Committee on Foreign Policy, the institute was created, in 1962, not as an act of labor, but of government (Kwitney 1985:341).

> Clearly, AIFLD's central functions are to combat noncapitalist influences within the ranks of Latin American labor . . . and to strengthen U.S. labor's influence and the U.S. business image in order to develop pro-capitalist, reformist unions while maintaining Latin America as a field of investment. (Spalding 1977:259)

Kwitney (1985) doubts that the average rank and file worker in the United States is aware of the institute and even less so of its activities. Uglow (circa 1986–87) says, with reference to the activities of the government and United States transnationals generally, "To the degree that massive immigration is regarded as undesirable, those activities and policies have not been in the United States' best interest." Clearly they have been in the best interest of corporate investors, for whom borders have relatively little meaning. "Capital is far more mobile than labor, and, instead of staying in the territory to fight it out, capital can escape, leaving labor with declining job opportunities and no way to protect itself" (Bonacich and Cheng 1984:25).

In the 1980s, attempts by some organizers and rank and file members in the labor movement to wrestle control away from an entrenched and conservative leadership escalated. The United Automobile Workers' (UAW) "New Directions," based in Detroit, and Teamsters for a Democratic Union (TDU) are perhaps two of the best known. Despite the changing character of the work force, increasingly minority and female, the top of the union hierarchy remains a white-male province. During the 1980s, the number and percentage of Latinos in the labor force grew dramatically. Immigration certainly explains a portion of this growth. The non-Latino work force grew by 10.4 percent between 1980 and 1987 and the Latino work force by 39 percent — and Latinas have shown the most rapid growth. Despite occupational upgrading in the Latino community, Latinos are still concentrated at the lower end of the occupational structure (Cattan 1988). The Latino labor force is expected to increase 74 percent between 1986 and the year 2000, which will make Latinos 10 percent of the labor force (from 7 percent in 1986) (Fullerton 1987).

The organizations noted in the preceding paragraph and others are attempting to democratize unions by making sure their leadership reflects, among other things, the changing ethnic and gender composition of the membership and by insuring that they take more progressive positions on domestic and foreign policy issues. The danger, warned some of the organizers, is that the predominantly conservative and white-male leadership may be replaced simply by less conservative white men, to the exclusion of racial and ethnic minorities and women.

Participation in a movement denotes numerous and quite different activities, and the perceived costs and benefits of each participant (or group of participants) can (and do) vary considerably (Klandermans 1984). The costs and benefits vary over time, between regions, industries, and sectors of the economy. All this affects the timing, strategies employed, and the arena. These considerations flag the need to consider crosscultural differences among workers and, consequently, signal the need for unions to employ and to have in important decision-making positions people conversant with the experiences and perceptions of African-Americans, Latinos, women, and immigrants.

My research suggests that the degree to which this segment of the work force can be unionized will be determined largely by organized labor's willingness, and capacity, to invest the necessary resources to organize these workers. Camagua is a case in point, but one that, as noted earlier, may be the exception that proves the rule. If, in order to organize workers in the secondary labor market, unions have to expend exorbitant amounts of financial and other resources, they may opt not to organize in these sectors of the economy. But, given the shift away from heavy manufacturing and toward the services and light manufacturing, especially marked in some regions and cities of the country, organized labor may be left with few, if any, alternatives.

Despite organized labor's reluctance to organize new immigrants from Europe in the early 1900s, their numbers alone made it impossible to ignore them. "Nativists had to choose between accepting the immigrants into their union or risking a severe loss of bargaining power" (Asher 1982:331). As one unionist remarked early in the twentieth century, " 'We organize them after they get here. . . . we don't bring them over here. . . . When they are in America, we are compelled to organize them in self-defense' " (quoted in Asher 1982:347–48). This sentiment is shared by many organizers in Los Angeles in the 1990s. The sheer number of undocumented workers in some regions and sectors of the country and economy, respectively, and the inability, and perhaps unwillingness, of the state to stop or even significantly reduce the number of undocumented immigrants entering the United States makes them impossible to ignore.

Camagua's workers, by their actions, accounts of their participation in an organizing campaign, and explanations of why they supported or did not support the unionization of the plant, forced me to rethink and then to challenge certain assumptions commonly held about the organizability — or rather, the unorganizability — of undocumented workers. But what occurred at Camagua transcended unionization. As Camagua's supervisor, Fernando González, observed, workers in the plant were changed by the experience: "No, before the union those women [nodding toward the sealing machines] wouldn't look at you. They were scared. They hardly talked. I didn't think they were intelligent. Now it's different. Now they look you in the eye and tell you *exactly* what they think. They're not the same."

Notes

Chapter I

1. The methodological problems inherent in counting a "fugitive" population such as this one are formidable. Hill (1985) does an excellent job of discussing some of these problems and reviewing a number of other attempts to come up with an accurate count of undocumented immigrants in the United States. Furthermore, the number of undocumented immigrants in the United States sometimes is purposely exaggerated or underestimated, depending on the political climate or the political agenda of the person or agency reporting the statistics.

2. With few exceptions, the names of these and other individuals, firms, and organizations appearing in this book are fictitious.

3. "Coyote" means smuggler — in this case, smuggler of people into the United States. For a fee, coyotes help immigrants enter the country without documents.

4. Other factors also said to contribute to labor's quandary are the effectiveness of employer resistance to unionization, the decline in heavy manufacturing and other industries with high levels of unionization, a rapid growth in traditionally nonunion sectors of the economy, an increase in part-time workers, a growth in jobs in geographic areas with low levels of unionization, employer-biased labor laws and lack of enforcement of laws protecting workers' rights, and organized labor's failure to organize more aggressively and militantly. These factors are of course not mutually exclusive. For example, the success employers have had in preventing the unionization of their workers is related to weak enforcement of labor laws protecting workers' rights. On the subject, see Edwards 1986; Edwards and Podgursky 1986; Freeman and Medoff 1984; Goldfield 1987.

5. See Averitt 1968; Bluestone 1970; Cain 1976; Doeringer and Piore 1971; Edwards, Reich, and Gordon 1975; Gordon, Edwards, and Reich 1982; and O'Connor 1973 on dual or segmented labor markets.

6. Among the reasons for unions' greater success historically in the core

are higher profits; increased costs, which are more easily passed on to consumers; and employers who are more likely to be tied to particular locations (Edwards and Podgursky 1986). Also, the organizing cost-per-worker incurred by a union is lower in larger, core firms, and the return in dues paid by workers is substantially greater.

7. Lane (1987:150) notes that in the early part of the century, restrictionists in the labor ranks emphasized the "tractable and passive character" of eastern and southern European immigrants. The fatalism attributed to these immigrants is not unlike the stereotype of the fatalistic or passive Latino, used by some to explain the unorganizability of these workers. The following excerpt from an article by Garza (1977:98) lays out the issue succinctly: "Fatalism and many other forms of passivity are cultural characteristics commonly attributed to Chicanos. . . . Most ethnographic and anthropological accounts depict Chicanos as passive — controlled by the external forces of luck, fate, and chance. This stereotypic characterization is practically identical to that attributed to Mexican nationals. Mexicans have been consistently characterized by the traits of passivity and subjugation." A number of social-psychological studies on the locus of control contradict the cultural stereotype of a passive and fatalistic orientation. As one group of researchers concluded after reviewing the literature and conducting their own research on locus of control, "Evidence to support a stereotype of a Mexican factory worker, a Mexican university student, or a Chicano high school senior as fatalistic, believing that his own actions are irrelevant to personal outcomes, is almost totally lacking" (Cole, Rodríguez, and Cole 1978:1328).

8. Earlier interviews with undocumented workers were conducted, for the most part, with apprehended immigrants awaiting deportation.

9. I was interested only in the participation of undocumented immigrants in organizing campaigns of previously unorganized firms. I concur with Bailey (1987), who notes that unionization rates are not very useful if they include undocumented immigrants who find jobs in closed union shops. For example, most of the large manufacturers of innerspring mattresses and furniture in Los Angeles, were organized before the major influx of Mexican and Central American immigrants into the industry in the sixties.

10. As Lijphart (1971:692n) notes, Marsh (1964:191) uses the term "specification" to refer to the "process of refining generalizations through deviant case analysis."

11. Arend Lijphart (1968) uses "amendments" to refer to modifications of extant theory in a deviant case study he conducted in the Netherlands.

12. "Migra" is the word immigrants often use to refer to either the border patrol or the Immigration and Naturalization Service.

13. The phrase "permanent settlement" is perhaps misleading since many of these long-term residents claim that they plan to return to Mexico. For all intents and purposes, however, many, if not most, do not return and even if they eventually do return, in the interim they make their home in the United States for an extended period.

14. The interview with the border patrol agent was relatively informal and took place over the course of a three-hour tour of the border, which I described in part earlier in this chapter. We observed the apprehension of several immigrants spotted by a helicopter and the pursuit of a coyote driving a car with six adults and five children as passengers, including two adults holding infants. The immigrants were apprehended, but the coyote scaled a fence and escaped.

15. The study focused on the period prior to the passage of the Immigration Reform and Control Act (IRCA) in 1986, but I discussed the impact of the new law with many of my respondents and between May and August of 1988 collected additional data on the impact of this new immigration amendment on organizing efforts. I discuss some of this in the two final chapters.

Chapter II

1. He and his family own 100 percent of the company's stock.

2. One concern expressed by some scholars is that undocumented workers have a negative impact on low-wage native workers, including blacks. Other scholars, such as Reischauer (1989), contend that the evidence thus far tends not to support the claim that undocumented immigration has had a negative effect on the employment situation of African-Americans. See Bean, Lowell, and Taylor 1988; Borjas 1983; Muller and Espenshade 1985.

3. Today the company's entire operations are housed under one roof, with the exception of warehouses. They moved to their new facility toward the end of the campaign.

4. I was able to speak with Hiram Ramírez on four different occasions, but his son Bob refused to speak with me. He did not trust me and would have preferred that I not speak with anyone.

5. See Edwards (1979:97–104) for a discussion of scientific management.

6. Moreno was hired on a temporary basis for the campaign. She had been a worker at a plant that closed down after she, her fellow workers, and the CWU refused to grant the concessions that management was demanding. After the plant closed down, the union concentrated on Camagua.

7. In fact, during my third visit to his house, he asked me a few questions about my methodology.

8. But while they constituted 75 percent of the membership of the International Ladies Garment Workers Union (ILGWU) in Los Angeles, they were not "integrated into union leadership positions" (Durón 1984:158).

9. For an excellent discussion on the subject, see chapter eleven in Freeman and Medoff (1984).

10. I was unable to secure the video from the CWU, but an organizer from the CWU indicated that their sessions with workers were almost identical to the one described in a United Electrical, Radio and Machine Workers Union (UE) guide.

11. This appeared in CWU's newsletter, issue no. 52, February–March 1986.

12. To the union's surprise, consumers of waterbeds were not overwhelmingly yuppies. A significant portion of the market was in the blue-collar sector.

13. The attorneys obviously had a financial stake, as well, in dragging out the campaign.

14. Ten cents on April 1, 1986, fifteen cents on September 1, 1986, and twenty cents on October 1, 1987.

15. One observer of southern California's labor scene and a former organizer questions the notion of a weak contract, arguing that most contracts are marked improvements over no contract. Nonetheless, even within this sector, the contract was relatively weak.

Chapter III

1. In Arizona's mines, Mexican and other workers struck in 1903, 1907, 1914, 1915, and 1917 (Foner 1982; Gómez-Quiñones 1972; Kluger 1970; Maciel 1981a, 1981b). As in the fields, owners, with the backing of local

police and vigilantes, managed in most cases to break the strikes. Yet in the 1915 Clifton-Moreci copper strikes, "strikebreakers, gunmen, militiamen, sheriffs, and their deputies — the usual array of forces relied upon by corporations in their battles with unions — could not be counted on . . . to bring about a settlement favorable to the mining corporations" (Foner 1982:21). Two-thirds or more of the strikers were Mexican. A year earlier, in the famous Ludlow, Colorado, ten-month strike against the Rockefeller-owned Colorado Fuel and Iron Company, vigilantes set fire to the strikers' makeshift camp and killed eighteen people, including five children (Gómez-Quiñones 1972:30; Maciel 1981b:142–43).

2. These two workers were involved in a campaign to organize the Roman Catholic diocese's cemetery workers in Los Angeles.

3. "Gabacho" is a mildly depreciative word used to refer to Anglos.

4. Latino organizations, and labor leaders in the United States and Mexico, criticized the action and rebutted the INS's and others' argument that these workers take jobs away from natives. They saw it as a ploy by the Reagan administration to divert attention from its failed policies by scapegoating immigrants (Stammer 1982:1).

5. For an excellent article on the stigmatization of jobs, see Oppenheimer 1974.

6. "The Texas Revolution of 1836 and the War of 1848 brought to the United States . . . half of the territory of the Mexican nation and three-quarters of its natural resources" (Gómez-Quiñones 1979:496). Today we know the territory as the states of Texas, California, Arizona, New Mexico, Utah, Nevada, and parts of Colorado and Wyoming. The Mexican government received fifteen million dollars in war indemnities through the Treaty of Guadalupe Hidalgo and an additional ten million dollars for the Valley of Mesilla (southern Arizona) with the Gadsden Purchase (Alba 1967:60–63; Cockcroft 1983:72).

7. In the decades immediately following the conquest, many of these people lost, largely by illegal means, an estimated twenty million acres of land (Cockcroft 1983:73). "By the turn of the century, Mexicans had been largely dispossessed of their property. Relegated to a lower-class status, they were overwhelmingly dispossessed landless laborers, politically and economically impotent" (Estrada et al. 1981:109).

8. There were many people — especially employers — who believed that Mexicans were particularly well suited, physically and psychologically, for agricultural labor. Reisler (1976:137–40) cites several examples of opin-

ions along these lines offered by farmers and politicians: A Texas congress-man, for example, speculated that by the "providence of God" the Mexi-can was adapted for "the burdensome task of bending his back to picking the cotton and the burdensome task of grubbing the fields." Hoffman (1974:10) cites the following remark by Dr. George P. Clements, who, in his defense of an open border, said that agriculture was something "to which the Oriental and Mexican due to their crouching and bending habits are fully adapted." In 1912, Stanford University professor Samuel Bryan (1912:730) wrote, "Their low standards of living and of morals, their illiteracy, their utter lack of proper political interest, the retarding effect of their employment upon the wage scale of the more progressive races, and finally their tendency to colonize in urban centers, with evil results, combine to stamp them as a rather undesirable class of residents." This statement illustrates the distinction often made between the desir-ability of some foreigners as workers, but not as citizens.

9. While undocumented workers have always been concentrated in the Southwest, by 1950 arrests of undocumented immigrants were being reported in virtually every state. In 1951, thirty-eight were arrested on the Alaska Railroad near the Arctic Circle (Hadley 1956:336).

10. Between 1920 and 1926, 329,269 Mexicans departed Mexico for the United States. During the same period, 557,718 returned, prompting Gamio (1971:7, 10) to comment that 228,449 returned "without first departing" from Mexico.

11. A bilateral international agreement between the executive branches of the Mexican and United States governments, the Emergency Labor Program was designed to fill wartime labor shortages with Mexican con-tract workers (see Galarza 1964; García y Griego 1983).

12. Even the immigrants themselves were sometimes surprised that their stay was more permanent than they had anticipated or planned. "The Mexican immigrant is usually conscious of his role in the United States, but seldom faces the probability that his migration is more perma-nent than he had intended. The expected return to Mexico continues to recede into the future while ties to the United States become stronger" (Taylor 1931:202). This was very much the case for many of the workers I interviewed in my study. On the question of docility, there are examples of employers' fears about the violent nature of Mexicans and seemingly contradictory statements, such as the following one by Victor Clark in

1908 (Clark 1974:496): "He is docile, patient, usually orderly in camp, fairly intelligent under competent supervision, obedient, and cheap. If he were active and ambitious, he would be less tractable and would cost more." Elsewhere, he writes that "the Mexicans are very tenacious of their rights" (Clark 1974:511).

13. "Settle" appears in quotation marks because "even among the most experienced, most integrated U.S. migrants . . . the permanence of settlement is rarely wholly certain" (Massey et al. 1987:274). Immigrants do not sever ties with family back home, nor do they abandon completely earlier intentions to return home. On the other hand, organizers generally smiled when they heard of long-term residents who talked about returning to Mexico. One organizer, with reference to one such statement by a worker he knew, commented: "Yeah, he has been going back for fifteen years."

14. A similar trend has been unfolding in western Europe during the past twenty to twenty-five years (Heisler and Heisler 1986).

15. Mark Granovetter (1982) makes the useful distinction between weak ties (ties with acquaintances) and strong ties (ties with family and close friends) and emphasizes the importance of the former for political organization and access to types of information not provided by the latter.

16. A second factor, the availability of individuals to participate, seems to be supported as well, but much less clearly.

17. The literature on reference groups and relative deprivation is instructive here. Runciman (1966:9), for example, writes, "The related notions of 'relative deprivation' and 'reference group' both derive from a familiar truism: that people's attitudes, aspirations and grievances largely depend on the frame of reference within which they are conceived." Also see Hyman and Singer 1968; and, for a review of the literature on reference groups, Schmitt 1972.

18. Leadmen make up the first level of supervision. They are part of the production work force, but are responsible for supervising a small group of workers. Though the owner referred to the leadmen in his comments, it was the abusive supervisory style of higher-level supervisors that evoked the ire of the workers.

19. Medical insurance was not more of a factor in the unionization of the plant because they already had a medical plan. In addition to ending the abusive treatment by supervisors and securing greater job security, wages seemed to be the only other issue that motivated workers appreciably.

20. These findings, however, are based on samples of white males.

21. This is not to say, of course, that slaves did not resist. Their resistance took many forms, including rebellions (Genovese 1979).

22. One worker recalled that when she joined the company in 1971 there were only twelve production workers.

23. The growth of the company also made it more susceptible to unionization because it was in a better position, financially, to "afford" a union. Less successful companies in this sector are often ignored by unions because they are not in a position to provide workers with very much in the way of wage increases and benefits.

Chapter IV

1. The data do not support him. For an excellent treatment of the issue, see Freeman and Medoff (1984). Interestingly, several of the other manufacturers I interviewed disagreed with Camagua's owner on this point.

2. Few of them have positions in the higher levels of the union structure. Several of the Latino organizers brought up this issue and expressed considerable anger and frustration with the failure of their respective unions to act on it affirmatively.

3. They claimed to have poured in $1.5 million, but Kersey placed the figure closer to Rivas's $500,000.

4. Also known as the Wagner Act, the NLRA was passed by Congress in July 1935. It gave workers the right to organize and reaffirmed their freedoms of speech, press, and assembly, which employers often denied. The FLSA was passed by Congress in 1939 and established minimum wages, required employers to pay overtime, and abolished certain types of child labor. See Yates (1987) for a concise review of United States labor laws.

5. Exceptions include agricultural workers, persons employed by their parents or spouse, supervisors, and domestics.

6. See Calavita (1982) for a concise and excellent account of the disappearance of this law.

7. Justices Rehnquist and Powell construed the NLRA to exclude undocumented immigrants.

8. In a recent two-to-one decision in *Del Rey Tortillería, Inc. v. NLRB* (1992), the Court of Appeals for the seventh circuit in effect agreed with Judge Beezer's dissenting opinion. In this case the seventh circuit rejected

the NLRB's petition for enforcement of its backpay order, holding that Bernardo Bravo and Nicolás Parédez (also known as Gorgonio Hernández), two workers discharged in violation of the NLRA by Del Rey Tortillería, Inc., were not entitled to backpay for any period of time during which they were in the country illegally. The court withdrew its decision, however, and a review by the full panel of judges of the seventh circuit is pending.

9. Vance referred to the ninth circuit court's interpretation of *Sure-Tan* on this issue in *Felbro*, but declined to express an opinion on it. In the same footnote, however, he wrote that the ninth circuit court "*narrowly*" (my emphasis) interpreted *Sure-Tan*.

10. Gibbs (1987) notes that in 1985, NLRB Associate General Counsel De Sio issued a memorandum (G.C. Memo OM 85–57, 85–89; 120 LRRM 342, 1985) requiring NLRB compliance officers, on the basis of the *Sure-Tan* decision, to investigate discriminatees' immigration status whenever it is raised by an employer.

11. The I-9 is used by the INS to verify a person's immigration status. All employees hired after November 6, 1986, must complete this form. Collyer also noted that it was not the intent of Congress to overrule *Sure-Tan* when it passed IRCA.

Chapter V

1. For a critique of the role of organizations in social protest see Piven and Cloward (1977).

2. Fantasia's (1988) analysis is based principally on his study of a strike by hospital workers.

3. In his study of the 1985 Columbia University divestment protest, Hirsch (1990:252) posits that theories of movement mobilization must consider how individuals are influenced by group-level processes to sacrifice self-interest: "Rational choice theories cannot explain why students joined and became committed to this protest action because group processes are not just the sum of individual preferences or predispositions." Similarly, Fantasia (1988:174) writes, "The actual process of mobilization is rarely the result of a multitude of individual responses and is shaped considerably by the collective chemistry of intragroup relations."

4. The other encounters listed are recruitment meetings, internal meetings, encounters with the media, encounters with allies, and encounters

with countermovement groups (Gamson, Fireman, and Rytina 1982:10–12).

5. Griffin, Wallace, and Rubin (1986) aver that collective action models should consider how capital disorganizes labor, that is, countermobilization by movement adversaries.

6. The role of discontents, or grievances, in collective action is a central issue in social movements research. Jenkins (1985), McCarthy and Zald (1977), Wilson (1973), and Jenkins and Perrow (1977) indicate that grievances are relatively constant and it is resources made available to aggrieved groups that explain fundamentally the emergence of a movement. In the Camagua case, as I have indicated, the resources provided by the union were critical, though not sufficient to explain the emergence and maintenance of the campaign.

7. The law does not require employers to ask for the documents of workers hired prior to November 6, 1986, but if they wish to, they can.

8. The cost of a fake document can run anywhere from ten to six hundred dollars, depending on the quality. Some workers simply rent them to secure a job under an alias (Cornelius 1988).

9. For some, of course, this concern may simply be a convenient justification to continue employing undocumented workers irrespective of what other employers do.

10. Goldfield (1987) notes that the decline has been a steady one since the mid-fifties.

11. While Delgado mentions agricultural labor, the majority of undocumented immigrants are nonagricultural workers toiling in urban areas.

12. This is from a draft of an undated article (circa 1986–87) by Margaret Uglow, obtained from the American Friends Service Committee. This particular quote is taken from pages 70 and 73 of the draft.

Bibliography

Acuña, Rodolfo. 1981. *Occupied America: A History of Chicanos.* New York: Harper & Row.

———. 1988. *Occupied America: A History of Chicanos.* New York: Harper & Row.

Adams, L. T. 1985. "Changing Employment Patterns of Organized Workers." *Monthly Labor Review* 108 (2):25–31.

AFL-CIO Committee on the Evolution of Work. 1985. *The Changing Situation of Workers and Their Unions.* Washington, D.C.: AFL-CIO.

Alba, Victor. 1967. *The Mexicans: The Making of a Nation.* New York: Frederick A. Praeger.

Alco Iron and Metal Co. 1984. 269 NLRB no. 87, slip op. at 5, 115 LRRM 1322.

Arroyo, Luis Leobardo. 1981. "Mexican Workers and American Unions: The Los Angeles AFL, 1890–1933." Chicano Political Economy Collective Working Paper Series, no. 107. Berkeley: Chicano Studies Library Publications, University of California.

Asher, Robert. 1982. "Union Nativism and the Immigrant Response." *Labor History* 23, no. 3 (Summer):325–48.

Averitt, Robert. 1968. *The Dual Economy.* New York: Norton.

Bailey, Thomas R. 1987. *Immigrant and Native Workers: Contrasts and Competition.* Boulder, Colo.: Westview Press.

Bean, Frank D., B. Lindsay Lowell, and Lowell J. Taylor. 1988. "Undocumented Mexican Immigrants and the Earnings of Other Workers in the United States." *Demography* 25, no. 1 (February):35–52.

Becklund, Laurie. 1984. "Fear Joins INS in Seeking Out Illegal Aliens at Work." *Los Angeles Times.* April 20, part 1.

———. 1985. "INS Holds 600 Illegal Aliens in Sweep of Six Job Locations." *Los Angeles Times.* June 6, part 2.

Berg, Bruce L. 1989. *Qualitative Research Methods for the Social Sciences.* Boston: Allyn and Bacon.

Bernstein, Harry. 1985. "Illegal Alien Issue Raised in East L.A. Dispute." *Los Angeles Times.* September 18, part 4.

Bevles Company, Inc., v. Teamsters Local 986. 1986. 791 F.2d 1391 (ninth circuit court).

Bluestone, Barry. 1970. "The Tripartite Economy: Labor Markets and the Working Poor." *Poverty and Human Resources Abstracts* 5:15–35.

Bodnar, John. 1982. *Workers' World: Kinship, Community, and Protest in an Industrial Society, 1900–1940.* Baltimore: Johns Hopkins University Press.

Bogardus, Emory S. 1934. *The Mexican in the United States.* Los Angeles: University of Southern California Press.

Bonacich, Edna, and Lucie Cheng. 1984. "Introduction: A Theoretical Orientation to International Labor Migration." In *Labor Immigration Under Capitalism: Asian Workers in the United States Before World War II,* edited by Lucie Cheng and Edna Bonacich, 1–56. Berkeley: University of California Press.

Borjas, George. 1983. "Substitutability of Black, Hispanic, and White Labor." *Economic Inquiry* 21 (January):93–106.

Briggs, Vernon M. 1978. "Labor Market Aspects of Mexican Migration to the United States in the 1970s." In *Views Across the Border: The United States and Mexico,* edited by Stanley R. Ross, 204–25. Albuquerque: University of New Mexico Press.

———. 1983. "Foreign Labor Programs as an Alternative to Illegal Immigration: A Dissenting View." In *The Border That Joins: Mexican Migrants and U.S. Responsibility,* edited by Peter G. Brown and Henry Shue, 223–45. Totowa, N.J.: Rowman and Littlefield.

Brody, David. 1960. *Steelworkers in America.* New York: Russell and Russell.

Browning, Harley L., and Néstor Rodríguez. 1985. "The Migration of Mexican Indocumentados as a Settlement Process: Implications for Work." In *Hispanics in the U.S. Economy,* edited by George J. Borjas and Marta Tienda, 277–97. Orlando, Fla.: Academic Press.

Bryan, Samuel. 1912. "Mexican Immigrants in the United States." *The Survey* 28, no. 23 (September 7):726–30.

Bustamante, Jorge A. 1973. "The Historical Context of Undocumented Mexican Immigrants to the United States." *Aztlan* 3, no. 2 (Fall):257–81.

Bustamante, Jorge A., and James D. Cockcroft. 1983. "Unequal Exchange in the Binational Relationship: The Case of Immigrant Labor." In *Mexican-U.S. Relations: Conflict and Convergence*, edited by Carlos Vásquez and Manuel García y Griego, 309–23. Los Angeles: University of California Chicano Studies Research Center Publications and Latin American Center Publications.

Cain, Glen G. 1976. "The Challenge of Segmented Labor Market Theories to Orthodox Theory: A Survey." *Journal of Economic Literature* 5, no. 14 (December):1215–57.

Calavita, Kitty. 1982. "California's 'Employer Sanctions': The Case of the Disappearing Law." Research Report Series, 39. La Jolla, Calif.: Center for U.S.-Mexican Studies, University of California, San Diego.

Cardoso, Lawrence A. 1980. *Mexican Emigration to the United States, 1897–1931: Socio-Economic Patterns*. Tucson: University of Arizona Press.

Cattan, Peter. 1988. "The Growing Presence of Hispanics in the U.S. Work Force." *Monthly Labor Review* 111, no. 8 (August):9–14.

Clark, Victor S. 1974. "Mexican Labor in the United States." In *Mexican Labor in the United States*, edited by Carlos E. Cortés, 466–522. New York: Arno Press

Cockcroft, James D. 1983. *Mexico: Class Formation, Capital Accumulation, and the State*. New York: Monthly Review Press.

———. 1986. *Outlaws in the Promised Land: Mexican Immigrant Workers and America's Future*. New York: Grove Press.

Cole, David, Jacqueline Rodríguez, and Shirley Cole. 1978. "Locus of Control in Mexicans and Chicanos: The Case of the Missing Fatalist." *Journal of Consulting and Clinical Psychology* 46, no. 6 (December):1323–29.

Collyer, Rosemary M. (general counsel, NLRB). 1987. Memorandum GC 87-8 on "The Impact of the Immigration Reform and Control Act of 1986 on Board Remedies for Undocumented Discriminatees." October 27.

———. 1988a. Memorandum GC 88-6 on "Reinstatement and Backpay Remedies for Undocumented Discriminatees." March 31.

———. 1988b. Memorandum GC 88-9 on "Reinstatement and Backpay Remedies for Discriminatees who are 'Undocumented Aliens.'" September 1.

Cooke, William N. 1985a. "The Rising Toll of Discrimination Against Union Activists." *Industrial Relations* 24, no. 3 (Fall):421–42.

————. 1985b. "The Failure to Negotiate First Contracts: Determinants and Policy Implications." *Industrial and Labor Relations Review* 38, no. 2 (January):163–78.

Cornelius, Wayne A. 1984. "The Role of Mexican Labor in the U.S. Economy: Two Generations of Research." Paper presented at the Annual Directors' Meeting of PROFMEX, the Consortium of U.S. Research Programs for Mexico. Cozumel, Mexico. July.

————. 1988. "Impacts of the 1986 Immigration Reform and Control Act: A Preliminary Assessment." Paper presented at the Thirty-ninth Annual Conference of the Council on Foundations. Los Angeles. April 6.

Cornelius, Wayne A., Leo R. Chávez, and Jorge G. Castro. 1982. "Mexican Immigrants and Southern California: A Summary of Current Knowledge." *Working Papers in U.S.-Mexican Studies*, no. 36. La Jolla, Calif.: Center for U.S.-Mexican Studies, University of California, San Diego.

Coyle, Laurie, Gail Hershatter, and Emily Honig. 1980. "Women at Farah: An Unfinished Story." In *Mexican Women in the United States*, edited by Magdalena Mora and Adelaida R. del Castillo, 117–44. Los Angeles: University of California, Chicano Research Center Publications.

Cummings, Scott. 1983. *Immigrant Minorities and the Urban Working Class*. Port Washington, N.Y.: Associated Faculty Press.

Daily Labor Report. 1990. no. 27 (February 8):8.

Daniel, Cletus E. 1981. *Bitter Harvest: A History of California Farmworkers, 1870–1941*. Ithaca, N.Y.: Cornell University Press.

Delgado, Gary. 1983. "Organizing Undocumented Workers." *Social Policy* 13, no. 4 (Spring):26–30.

Del Rey Tortillería, Inc. v. NLRB. 1992. 970. F.2d 262 (seventh circuit court).

Doeringer, Peter B., and Michael J. Piore. 1971. *Internal Labor Markets and Manpower Analysis.* Lexington, Mass.: D. C. Heath.

Dolores Canning Company, Inc., v. Howard (California Labor Commissioner). 1974. 40 Cal. App. 3d 673.

Durón, Clementina. 1984. "Mexican Women and Labor Conflict in Los Angeles: The ILGWU Dressmakers' Strike of 1933." *Aztlan* 15, no. 1 (Spring):145–61.

Edwards, Richard. 1979. *Contested Terrain: The Transformation of the Workplace in the Twentieth Century.* New York: Basic Books.

———. 1986. "Unions in Crisis and Beyond: Introduction." In *Unions in Crisis and Beyond: Perspectives from Six Countries*, edited by Richard Edwards, Paolo Garonna, and Franz Todtling, 1–13. Dover, Mass.: Auburn House Publishing.

Edwards, Richard, and Michael Podgursky. 1986. "The Unraveling Accord: American Unions in Crisis." In *Unions in Crisis and Beyond: Perspectives from Six Countries*, edited by Richard Edwards, Paolo Garonna, and Franz Todtling, 14–60. Dover, Mass.: Auburn House Publishing.

Edwards, Richard, Michael Reich, and David Gordon, eds. 1975. *Labor Market Segmentation*. Lexington, Mass.: Lexington Books.

Estrada, Leobardo F., F. Chris García, Reynaldo Flores Macías, and Lionel Maldonado. 1981. "Chicanos in the United States: A History of Exploitation and Resistance." *Daedalus* 110, no. 2 (Spring):103–31.

Executive, The. 1987. (February):84.

Fantasia, Rick. 1988. *Cultures of Solidarity: Consciousness, Action, and Contemporary American Workers*. Berkeley: University of California Press.

Fenton, Edwin. 1975. *Immigrants and Unions, A Case Study: Italians and American Labor, 1870–1920*. New York: Arno Press.

Ferree, Myra Marx, and Frederick D. Miller. 1985. "Mobilization and Meaning: Toward an Integration of Social Psychological and Resource Perspectives on Social Movements." *Sociological Inquiry*. 55, no. 1 (Winter):38–61.

Fiorito, Jack, and Charles R. Greer. 1982. "Determinants of U.S. Unionism: Past Research and Future Needs." *Industrial Relations* 21, no. 1 (Winter):1–32.

Fireman, Bruce, and William A. Gamson. 1988. "Utilitarian Logic in the Resource Mobilization Perspective." In *The Dynamics of Social Movements: Resource Mobilization, Social Control, and Tactics.* edited by Mayer N. Zald and John D. McCarthy, 8–44. Lanham, Md.: University Press of America.

Fogel, Walter. 1978. *Mexican Illegal Aliens in the United States*. Los Angeles: Institute of Industrial Relations, University of California.

Foner, Philip S. 1981. *Organized Labor and the Black Worker 1619–1981*. New York: International Publishers.

———. 1982. *History of the Labor Movement in the United States*. Vol. 6, *On the Eve of America's Entrance into World War I, 1915–1916*. New York: International Publishers.

Freedman, Marcia. 1985. "Urban Labor Markets and Ethnicity: Segments and Shelters Re-examined." In *Urban Ethnicity in the United States: New Immigrants and Old Minorities*, edited by Lionel Maldonado and Joan Moore, 145–65. Beverly Hills, Calif.: Sage Publications.

Freeman, Richard B., and James L. Medoff. 1984. *What Do Unions Do?* New York: Basic Books.

Fullerton, Howard N., Jr. 1987. "Labor Force Projections: 1986 to 2000." *Monthly Labor Review* 110, no. 9 (September):19–29.

Galarza, Ernesto. 1964. *Merchants of Labor: The Mexican Bracero Story*. San Jose, Calif.: Rosicrucian Press.

Galenson, Walter. 1986. "The Historical Role of American Trade Unionism." In *Unions in Transition: Entering the Second Century*, edited by Seymour Martin Lipset, 39–73. San Francisco: ICS Press.

Gamio, Manuel. 1971. *Mexican Immigration to the United States: A Study of Human Migration and Adjustment*. New York: Dover Publications. Unabridged republication. Chicago: University of Chicago Press, 1930.

Gamson, William A., Bruce Fireman, and Steven Rytina. 1982. *Encounters with Unjust Authority*. Homewood, Ill.: Dorsey Press.

García, Juan Ramón. 1980. *Operation Wetback: The Mass Deportation of Mexican Undocumented Workers in 1954*. Westport, Conn.: Greenwood Press.

García y Griego, Manuel. 1983. "The Importation of Mexican Contract Laborers to the United States, 1942–1964: Antecedents, Operation, and Legacy." In *The Border That Joins*, edited by Peter G. Brown and Henry Shue, 49–98. Totowa, N.J.: Rowman and Littlefield.

Garza, Raymond T. 1977. "Personal Control and Fatalism in Chicanos and Anglos: Conceptual and Methodological Issues." In *Chicano Psychology*, edited by Joe L. Martinez, Jr., 97–108. New York: Academic Press.

Genovese, Eugene D. 1974. *Roll, Jordan, Roll: The World the Slaves Made*. New York: Pantheon Books.

———. 1976. *From Rebellion to Revolution: Afro-American Slave Revolts in the Making of the New World*. New York: Vintage Books.

Gibbs, Robert H. 1987. "Unions and the Immigration Reform and Control Act of 1986." Paper presented at a seminar on Representing and Counseling Undocumented Workers. Whittier School of Law, Los Angeles.

Giddens, Anthony. 1984. *The Constitution of Society: Outline of the Theory of Structuration*. Cambridge, Mass.: Polity.

Goldfield, Michael. 1987. *The Decline of Organized Labor in the United States*. Chicago: University of Chicago Press.

Gómez-Quiñones, Juan. 1970. "Research Notes on the Twentieth Century: Notes on Periodization 1900–1965." *Aztlan* 1, no. 1 (Spring): 115–23.

———. 1972. "The First Steps: Chicano Labor Conflict and Organizing 1900–1920." *Aztlan* 3, no. 1 (Spring):13–49.

———. 1979. "The Origins and Development of the Mexican Working Class in the United States: Laborers and Artisans North of the Rio Bravo, 1600–1900." In *Labor and Laborers Through Mexican History*, edited by Elsa Cecilia Frost, Michael C. Meyer, Josefina Zoraida Vázquez in collaboration with Lilia Díaz, 463–505. Mexico: El Colegio de Mexico.

González, Josie M. 1988. "The Management Perspective." *Industrial Relations Law Journal* 10 (1):111–15.

Gordon, David. 1972. *Theories of Poverty and Unemployment: Orthodox, Radical, and Dual Labor Market Perspectives*. Lexington, Mass.: D. C. Heath.

Gordon, David, Richard Edwards, and Michael Reich. 1982. *Segmented Work, Divided Workers*. New York: Cambridge University Press.

Granovetter, Mark. 1982. "The Strength of Weak Ties: A Network Theory Revisited." In *Social Structure and Network Analysis*, edited by Peter V. Marsden and Nan Lin, 105–30. Beverly Hills, Calif.: Sage Publications.

Griffin, Larry J., Michael E. Wallace, and Beth A. Rubin. 1986. "Capitalist Resistance to the Organization of Labor Before the New Deal: Why? How? Success?" *American Sociological Review* 51, no. 2 (April):147–67.

Hadley, Eleanor M. 1956. "A Critical Analysis of the Wetback Problem." *Law and Contemporary Problems* 21, no. 2 (Spring):334–57.

Heisler, Barbara Schmitter, and Martin O. Heisler. 1986. "Transnational Migration and the Modern Democratic State: Familiar Problems in New Form or a New Problem?" *Annals of the American Academy of Political and Social Science* 485 (May):12–22.

Heneman Herbert III, and Marcus H. Sandver. 1983. "Predicting the Outcome of Union Certification Elections: A Review of the Literature." *Industrial and Labor Relations Review* 36, no. 4 (July):537–59.

Higham, John. 1955. *Strangers in the Land: Patterns of American Nativism, 1860–1925*. New Brunswick, N.J.: Rutgers University Press.

Hill, Kenneth. 1985. "Illegal Aliens: An Assessment." In *Immigration Statistics: A Story of Neglect*, edited by Daniel B. Levine, Kenneth Hill, and Robert Warren, 225–54. Washington, D.C.: National Academy Press.

Hirsch, Eric L. 1990. "Sacrifice for the Cause: Group Processes, Recruitment, and Commitment in a Student Social Movement." *American Sociological Review* 55, no. 2 (April):243–54.

Hoffman, Abraham. 1974. *Unwanted Mexican Americans in the Great Depression: Repatriation Pressures, 1929–1939*. Tucson: University of Arizona Press.

Hourwich, Isaac. 1912. *Immigration and Labour.* New York: G. P. Putnam and Sons.

Hyman, Herbert H., and Eleanor Singer, eds. 1968. *Readings in Reference Group Theory and Research.* New York: Free Press.

In re Reyes. 1987. 814 F.2d 168 (fifth circuit court).

INS v. Adan López-Mendoza et al. 1984. 468 U.S. 1032, 82 L. Ed. 2d 778, 104 S. Ct. 3479.

Jamieson, Stuart. 1976. *Labor Unionism in American Agriculture.* New York: Arno Press.

Jenkins, J. Craig. 1978. "The Demand for Immigrant Workers: Labor Scarcity or 'Social Control?'" *International Migration Review* 12, no. 4 (Winter):514–35.

———. 1985. *The Politics of Insurgency: The Farm Worker Movement in the 1960s.* New York: Columbia University Press.

Jenkins, J. Craig, and Charles Perrow. 1977. "Insurgency of the Powerless: Farm Worker Movements, 1946–1972." *American Sociological Review* 42, no. 2 (April):249–68.

Kistler, Alan. 1984. "Union Organizing: New Challenges and Prospects." *Annals of the American Academy of Political and Social Science* 473 (May):96–107.

Klandermans, Bert. 1984. "Mobilization and Participation: Social-Psychological Expansions of Resource Mobilization Theory." *American Sociological Review* 49, no. 5 (October):583–600.

Kluger, James R. 1970. *The Clifton-Morenci Strike: Labor Difficulty in Arizona, 1915–1916.* Tucson: University of Arizona Press.

Kochan, Thomas A. 1979. "How American Workers View Labor Unions." *Monthly Labor Review* 102, no. 4 (April):23–31.

Kokkelenberg, Edward C., and Donna R. Sockell. 1985. "Union Membership in the United States, 1973–1981." *Industrial and Labor Relations* 38, no. 4 (July):497–543.

Kuttner, Robert. 1987. "Will Unions Organize Again?" *Dissent* (Winter):52–62.

Kwitney, Jonathan. 1985. *Endless Enemies: The Making of an Unfriendly World*. New York: Congdon & Weed.

Lane, A. T. 1987. *Solidarity and Survival: American Labor and European Immigrants, 1830–1924*. New York: Greenwood Press.

Lawson, Tony. 1981. "Paternalism and Labour Market Segmentation Theory." In *The Dynamics of Labour Market Segmentation*, edited by Frank Wilkinson, 47–66. London: Academic Press.

Lehto, Bill. 1985. "Waterbed Dispute Continues." *Camarillo Daily News*. August 20.

Lijphart, Arend. 1968. *The Politics of Accommodation: Pluralism and Democracy in the Netherlands*. Berkeley: University of California Press.

——. 1971. "Comparative Politics and the Comparative Method." *American Political Science Review* 65, no. 3 (September):682–93.

Lipset, Seymour Martin, Martin A. Trow, and James S. Coleman. 1956. *Union Democracy: The Internal Politics of the International Typographical Union*. New York: Free Press.

Lipshultz, Robert J. 1962. "American Attitudes Toward Mexican Immigration, 1924–1952." Ph.D. diss., University of Chicago.

Local 512, Warehouse and Office Workers' Union, ILGWU, AFL-CIO, et al. v. NLRB. 1986. 795 F.2d 705 (ninth circuit court).

Lockwood, Charles, and Christopher B. Leinberger. 1988. "Los Angeles Comes of Age." *Atlantic Monthly* 261, no. 1 (January):31–56.

McAdam, Doug. 1982. *Political Process and the Development of Black Insurgency, 1930–1970*. Chicago: University of Chicago Press.

——. 1983. "Tactical Innovation and the Pace of Insurgency." *American Sociological Review* 48, no. 6 (December):735–54.

McCarthy, John D., and Mayer N. Zald. 1977. "Resource Mobilization and Social Movements." *American Journal of Sociology* 82, no. 6 (May):1212–41.

McCarthy, Kevin F., and R. Burciaga Valdéz. 1985. *Current and Future Effects of Mexican Immigration in California: Executive Summary*. Santa Monica: Rand Corporation.

Maciel, David. 1981a. *La clase obrera en la historia de México: Al norte del Río Bravo (pasado inmediato) (1930–1981)*. México: Siglo Veintiuno Editores.

———. 1981b. "Luchas Laborales y Conflictos de Clase de los Trabajadores Mexicanos en los Estados Unidos, 1900–1930." In *La clase obrera en la historia de México: Al norte de Río Bravo (pasado lejano) (1600–1930)*, edited by Juan Gómez-Quiñones and David Maciel, 89–217. Mexico: Siglo Veintiuno Editores.

McWilliams, Carey. 1939. *Factories in the Field: The Story of Migratory Farm Labor in California*. Boston: Little, Brown.

———. 1968. *North from Mexico: The Spanish-speaking People of the United States*. New York: Greenwood Press.

Maram, Sheldon L., with the assistance of Stuart Long and Dennis Berg. 1980. "Hispanic Workers in the Garment and Restaurant Industries in Los Angeles County." *Working Papers in U.S.-Mexican Studies*, no. 12. La Jolla: Center for U.S.-Mexican Studies, University of California, San Diego.

Marsh, Robert M. 1964. "The Bearing of Comparative Analysis on Sociological Theory." *Social Forces* 43, no. 2 (December):188–96.

Massey, Douglas S. 1985. "The Settlement Process Among Mexican Migrants to the United States: New Methods and Findings." In *Immigration Statistics: A Story of Neglect*, edited by Daniel B. Levine, Kenneth Hill, and Robert Warren, 255–89. Washington, D.C.: National Academy Press.

Massey, Douglas S., Rafael Alarcón, Jorge Durand, and Humberto González. 1987. *Return to Aztlan: The Social Process of International Migration from Western Mexico*. Berkeley: University of California Press.

Merton, Robert K. 1959. "Notes on Problem-Finding in Sociology." In *Sociology Today: Problems and Prospects*, edited by Robert K. Merton, Leonard Broom, and Leonard S. Cottrell, Jr., ix–xxxiv. New York: Basic Books.

Mexican American Legal Defense and Educational Fund (MALDEF). 1985. Brief Amici Curiae in *Local 512, Warehouse and Office Workers Union, ILGWU, AFL-CIO, et al. v. NLRB*. September 30.

Mexicans in California. 1930. Report of Gov. C. C. Young's Mexican Fact-Finding Committee (October). San Francisco: State Building.

Mines, Richard, and Michael Kaufman. 1985. "Mexican Immigrants: The Labor Market Issues." In *Mexico and the United States: Studies in Eco-*

nomic Interaction, edited by Peggy B. Musgrave, 207–28. Boulder, Colo.: Westview Press.

Moore, Barrington. 1978. *Injustice*. White Plains, N.Y.: Sharpe.

Mora, Magdalena. 1981. "The Tolteca Strike: Mexican Women and the Struggle for Union Representation." In *Mexican Immigrant Workers in the U.S.*, edited by Antonio Ríos-Bustamante, 111–17. Anthology no. 2. Los Angeles: University of California Chicano Studies Research Center Publications.

Muller, Thomas, and Thomas J. Espenshade. 1985. *The Fourth Wave: California's Newest Immigrants*. Washington, D.C.: Urban Institute Press.

NLRB v. Apollo Tire Co., Inc. 1979. 604 F.2d 1180 (ninth circuit court).

NLRB v. Ashkenazy Property Management Corporation. 1987. 817 F.2d 74 (ninth circuit court).

NLRB v. Sure-Tan, Inc. 1978. 583 F.2d 355 (seventh circuit court).

North, Douglas S., and Marion F. Houstoun. 1976. *The Characteristics and Role of Illegal Aliens in the U.S. Labor Market*. Washington, D.C.: Litton.

O'Connor, James. 1973. *The Fiscal Crisis of the State*. New York: St. Martin's Press.

Olivares, Jaime. 1983. "Polemica nacional por la actitud del jefe de policia de Santa Ana." *La Opinión* (October 24):2.

Olson, Mancur. 1977. *The Logic of Collective Action: Public Goods and the Theory of Groups*. Cambridge, Mass.: Harvard University Press.

Oppenheimer, Martin. 1974. "The Sub-Proletariat: Dark Skins and Dirty Work." *The Insurgent Sociologist* 4, no. 2 (Winter):7–20.

Otero, J. F. 1981. "Immigration Policy: Drifting Toward Disaster." *The AFL-CIO American Federationist* 88, no. 2 (February):1–6.

Passel, Jeffrey. 1986. "Undocumented Immigration." *Annals of the American Academy of Political and Social Sciences* 487 (September):181–200.

Passel, Jeffrey S., and Karen A. Woodrow. 1984. "Geographic Distribution of Undocumented Immigrants: Estimates of Undocumented Aliens Counted in the 1980 Census by State." *International Migration Review* 18, no. 3 (Fall):642–71.

Patel v. Quality Inn South. 1988. 846 F.2d 700 (eleventh circuit court).

Patel v. Sumani Corp., Inc. 1987. 660 F.Supp. 1528 (N.D. Ala.).

Perrow, Charles. 1988. "The Sixties Observed." In *The Dynamics of Social Movements: Resource Mobilization, Social Control, and Tactics*, edited by Mayer N. Zald and John D. McCarthy, 192–211. Lanham, Md.: University Press of America.

Pesotta, Rose. 1944. *Bread upon the Waters.* New York: Dodd, Mead.

Petzinger, Thomas, Jr., Mark Zieman, Bryan Burrough, and Dianna Solis. 1985. "Illegal Immigrants Are the Backbone in the States of the Southwest." *Wall Street Journal.* May 7.

Piore, Michael T. 1975. "Notes for a Theory of Labor Market Stratification." In *Labor Market Segmentation,* edited by Richard Edwards, Michael Reich, and David Gordon, 125–50. Lexington, Mass.: D. C. Heath.

———. 1979. *Birds of Passage: Migrant Labor and Industrial Societies.* Cambridge, Eng.: Cambridge University Press.

———. 1986. "The Shifting Grounds for Immigration." *Annals of the American Academy of Political and Social Science* 485 (May):23–33.

Piven, Frances Fox, and Richard A. Cloward. 1977. *Poor People's Movements: Why They Succeed, How They Fail.* New York: Vintage Books.

Poitras, Guy. 1980. *International Migration to the United States from Costa Rica and El Salvador.* San Antonio: Border Research Institute.

Portes, Alejandro. 1978. "Toward a Structural Analysis of Illegal (Undocumented) Immigration." *International Migration Review* 12, no. 4 (Winter):469–84.

Portes, Alejandro, and Robert L. Bach. 1985. *Latin Journey: Cuban and Mexican Immigrants in the United States.* Berkeley: University of California Press.

Reischauer, Robert D. 1989. "Immigration and the Underclass," *The Annals of the American Academy of Political and Social Sciences* 501 (January):120–31.

Reisler, Mark. 1974. "Passing Through Our Egypt: Mexican Labor in the United States, 1900–1940." Ph.D. diss., University of Michigan.

———. 1976. *By the Sweat of Their Brow: Mexican Immigrant Labor in the United States, 1900–1940.* Westport, Conn.: Greenwood Press.

Ríos v. Enterprise Association Steamfitters Local Union 638 of UA. 1988. 860 F.2d 1168 (second circuit court).

Roberts, Markley. 1984. "The Future Demographics of American Unionism." *Annals of the American Academy of Political and Social Science* 473 (May):23–32.

Romo, Ricardo. 1975. "Responses to Mexican Immigration, 1910–1930." *Aztlan* 6 (2):173–94.

Rosenblum, Gerald. 1973. *Immigrant Workers: Their Impact on American Labor Radicalism.* New York: Basic Books.

Rotella, Sebastian. 1992. "INS Agents Abuse Immigrants, Study Says." *Los Angeles Times*. May 31.

Rothstein, Richard. 1986. "L.A.'s Economy Depends on 'Illegals': Industries that Lose Low-Wage Workers Will Go Abroad," *Los Angeles Times*. November 23, part 5.

Ruiz, Vicki L. 1990. "A Promise Fulfilled: Mexican Cannery Workers in Southern California." In *Unequal Sisters: A Multi-cultural Reader in U.S. Women's History*, edited by Ellen Carol DuBois and Vicki L. Ruiz, 264–74. New York: Routledge.

Runciman, W. G. 1966. *Relative Deprivation and Social Justice: A Study of Attitudes to Social Inequality in Twentieth-Century England*. Berkeley: University of California Press.

Samora, Julian. 1971. *Los Mojados: The Wetback Story*. Notre Dame: University of Notre Dame Press.

Schmitt, Raymond L. 1972. *The Reference Other Orientation: An Extension of the Reference Group Concept*. Carbondale: Southern Illinois University Press.

Scott, James C. 1985. *Weapons of the Weak: Everyday Forms of Peasant Resistance*. New Haven, Conn.: Yale University Press.

Snow, David A., Louis A. Zurcher, Jr., and Sheldon Ekland-Olson. 1980. "Social Networks and Social Movements: A Microstructural Approach to Differential Recruitment." *American Sociological Review* 45, no. 5 (October):787–801.

Soja, Edward, Rebecca Morales, and Goetz Wolff. 1983. "Urban Restructuring: An Analysis of Social and Spatial Change in Los Angeles." *Economic Geography* 59, no. 2 (April):195–230.

Spalding, Jr., Hobart A. 1977. *Organized Labor in Latin America: Historical Case Studies of Workers in Dependent Societies*. New York: New York University Press.

Stammer, Larry. 1982. "INS Ends Raids on Illegal Aliens: 6,000 Seized in Week-Long Project." *Los Angeles Times*. May 1, part 1.

Stammer, Larry, and Victor M. Valle. 1982. "Most Aliens in Raids Back on Job: Survey Contradicts INS Findings That Sweeps Worked." *Los Angeles Times*. August 1, part 1.

Statistical Yearbook of the Immigration and Naturalization Service. 1984. U.S. Department of Justice, Immigration and Naturalization Service ENF 1.4, pp. 194–95.

Sure-Tan, Inc. v. NLRB. 1984. 467 U.S. 883, 81 L. Ed. 2d 732, 104 S. Ct. 2803.

Taylor, Paul, 1931. "Mexicans North of the Rio Grande." *The Survey* 66, no. 3 (May 1):135–205.

Tempest, Rone. 1982. "Houston Hard Pressed to Fill Aliens' Jobs." *Los Angeles Times.* May 1, part 1.

Thomas, Robert J. 1982. "Citizenship and Gender in Work Organization: Some Considerations for Theories of the Labor Process." In *Marxist Inquiries: Studies of Labor, Class, and States*, edited by Michael Burawoy and Theda Skocpol, 86–112. Chicago: University of Chicago Press.

———. 1985. *Citizenship, Gender, and Work: Social Organization of Industrial Agriculture.* Berkeley: University of California Press.

Uglow, Margaret. Circa 1986–87. "The National Interest and Immigration: A Re-Evaluation." Undated document obtained from the American Friends Service Committee.

U.S. Congress. House. *Immigration Reform and Control Act of 1986.* 99th Cong., 2d sess. October 14 (to accompany S. 1200).

U.S. Congress. H.R. 99–682, part 1. 1986. 99th Cong. 2d sess., 58.

U.S. Congress. H.R. 99–682, part 2. 1986. 99th Cong. 2d sess., 8.

U.S. Congress. National Labor Relations Act (NLRA). 1935. As amended, 29 U.S.C. Section 151 et seq.

Waldinger, Roger. 1986. *Through the Eye of the Needle: Immigrants and Enterprise in New York's Garment Trades.* New York: New York University.

Wallace, Steven P. 1986. "Central American and Mexican Immigrant Characteristics and Economic Incorporation in California." *International Migration Review* 20, no. 3 (Fall):657–71.

Weber, Devra Anne. 1973. "The Organizing of Mexicano Agricultural Workers: Imperial Valley and Los Angeles 1928–34, An Oral History Approach." *Aztlan* 3, no. 2 (Fall):307–47.

Wilson, John. 1973. *An Introduction to Social Movements.* New York: Basic Books.

Wollenberg, Charles. 1969. "Huelga, 1928 Style: The Imperial Valley Cantaloupe Workers' Strike." *Pacific Historical Review* 38, no. 1 (February):45–58.

———. 1975. "Working on El Traque: The Pacific Electric Strike of 1903." In *The Chicano*, edited by Norris Hundley, Jr., 96–107. Santa Barbara, Calif.: Clio Books.

Yates, Michael. 1987. *Labor Law Handbook*. Boston: South End Press.

Zavella, Patricia. 1987. *Women's Work and Chicano Families: Cannery Workers of the Santa Clara Valley*. Ithaca, N.Y.: Cornell University Press.

Zurcher, Louis A., and David A. Snow. 1981. "Collective Behavior: Social Movements." In *Social Psychology: Sociological Perspectives*, edited by Morris Rosenberg and Ralph H. Turner, 447–82. New York: Basic Books.

Index